P9-CEV-170

The Splendor of
ITALY
A Portrait in Pictures

Natasha Foges

E Splendor of

TALY

ortrait in Pictures

METRO BOOKS
New York

An Imprint of Sterling Publishing
387 Park Avenue South
New York, NY 10016

This 2012 edition published by Metro Books by
arrangement with Dorling Kindersley Limited.

DORLING KINDERSLEY

Author & executive editor

Natasha Foges

Publisher

Andrew Lockett

Editors

Ian Blenkinsop, Tracy
Hopkins, Joe Staines,
Michele Wells

Picture research

Ian Blenkinsop, Tracy
Hopkins, Diana Jarvis,
Andrew Lockett, Joe Staines

Designer

Diana Jarvis

Production

Gemma Sharpe,
Rebecca Short

ISBN 978-1-4351-3909-1

For information about custom editions, special sales,
and premium and corporate purchases, please contact
Sterling Special Sales at 800-805-5489 or
specialsales@sterlingpublishing.com.

Manufactured in China

2 4 6 8 10 9 7 5 3 1

www.sterlingpublishing.com

Contents

THE SPLENDOR OF ITALY

Introduction

With more World Heritage Sites selected for "outstanding universal value" than any other country in the world, Italy is iterally a spectacular country—a feast for the eyes. *The Splendor of Italy* attempts to capture the wonders on offer in a series of visual portraits organized in terms of the country's regions.

Natural wonders are abundant: picturesque mountains, volcanoes, lakes, and glorious rugged coastline. Within what are now Italian shores are many of the finest monuments of Classical civilization both Roman and Greek, and the inspiration for many of the outstanding achievements of the Renaissance—painting, sculpture, architecture, and landscaping. Yet the beauty of Italy is that its attractions are not confined to such major tourist destinations as Rome, Venice, or Florence—fantastic though they are—but can be found the length and the breadth of the country from Piemonte to Puglia, and from Trento to Tropea. Though Tuscany or one of the major cities may command the most attention in Italy and in these pages, you will never be too far away from a captivating hill town, an arresting palazzo, or a stunning coastline. Even if the phrase "a iving museum" is too sweeping an expression, the local character unique to each region makes the experience of visiting Italy a vital one: the finest scenery of the country literally makes many a traveler glad to be alive. *La Dolce Vita*, the "good life", is here.

With so many memorable sights to choose from, the selection of pictures to represent the diversity of the country has been a difficult but inspiring task. This book presents recent images of some famous and celebrated views, as well as others a little more off the beaten track but nonetheless special for that. Even f everybody's personal favorite is not represented in these pages, for most readers exciting new discoveries will be made. *Godetevi la vista*—enjoy the view!

Northern Italy

Trentino-Alto Adige • The Veneto • Friuli-Venezia Giulia
Lombardy • The Lakes
Piemonte • Valle d'Aosta • Liguria
Emilia-Romagna

NORTHERN ITALY

Trentino-Alto Adige
The Veneto
Friuli-Venezia Giulia

Northeastern Italy is a region of contrasts, from the majestic Dolomite mountains to the grand canals of one of the world's most famous cities. In lofty Trentino-Alto Adige, bordering Austria, nature's breathtaking vistas capture the eye, and the beautifully situated towns of Bolzano and Trento make the most of their splendid locations. In the Veneto region, Padua and handsome Verona, with its magnificent Roman arena, are known for their fine architecture and rich histories, but it is glorious Venice that steals the show. From grand St. Mark's Square, at risk of sinking back into the sea, to the graceful gondolas slipping quietly along the narrowest side-canals, Venice has an enduring appeal. The varied small towns of Italy's far northeast, including Udine, are also replete with exquisite historic buildings, fine piazzas and arresting statues dating from Roman to Renaissance times.

BOLZANO

The capital of Alto Adige sits in a sunny, sheltered valley at the junction of two rivers. It's also at the crossroads of two cultures—Italian and Austrian—and has a large German-speaking population which gives this unique market town much of its Tyrolean character. The surrounding countryside is excellent trekking territory, and three cable cars run from Bolzano to some of the spectacular surrounding peaks.

THE DOLOMITES

(previous pages)

In the shadow of the Geisler Spitzen peaks in the Italian Dolomites, sits the picture-postcard Vilnöss Valley. Sleepy hamlets, scattered farmhouses, and vineyards give this largely German-speaking region a timeless air of rural tranquility, absorbing the large number of walkers, climbers, and alpinists with ease.

MARMOLADA AND SASSO LUNGO MOUNTAINS

(opposite)

The jagged peak of Sasso Lungo provides a breathtaking sight for intrepid hikers taking the bucket lift up Marmolada, the highest of the Dolomite mountains (10,968 feet). The large Marmolada glacier was turned into a front-line "city of ice" during World War I when Austrian soldiers built an extensive network of caves and tunnels beneath it.

PIAZZA DEL DUOMO, TRENTO

(*opposite*)

A beautifully situated town encircled by mountains, Trento is famous for its eighteenth-century statue of Neptune (the Roman god of the sea) that dominates the central piazza. On two sides of the piazza, the Romanesque Duomo, with its medieval crypt, and the Palazzo Pretorio, with its fishtail battlements, help make this the most attractive town in the Trentino region.

PASSO DELLO STELVIO

(*below*)

With its 48 hairpin turns, the Stelvio Pass makes for an unforgettable journey across the Ortles mountains in the Eastern Alps as you cross from Switzerland into Northern Italy. As beloved by motorbikers as it is revered by cyclists (the Pass is regularly a key climb in the Giro d'Italia), it certainly ranks as one of Europe's great driving experiences.

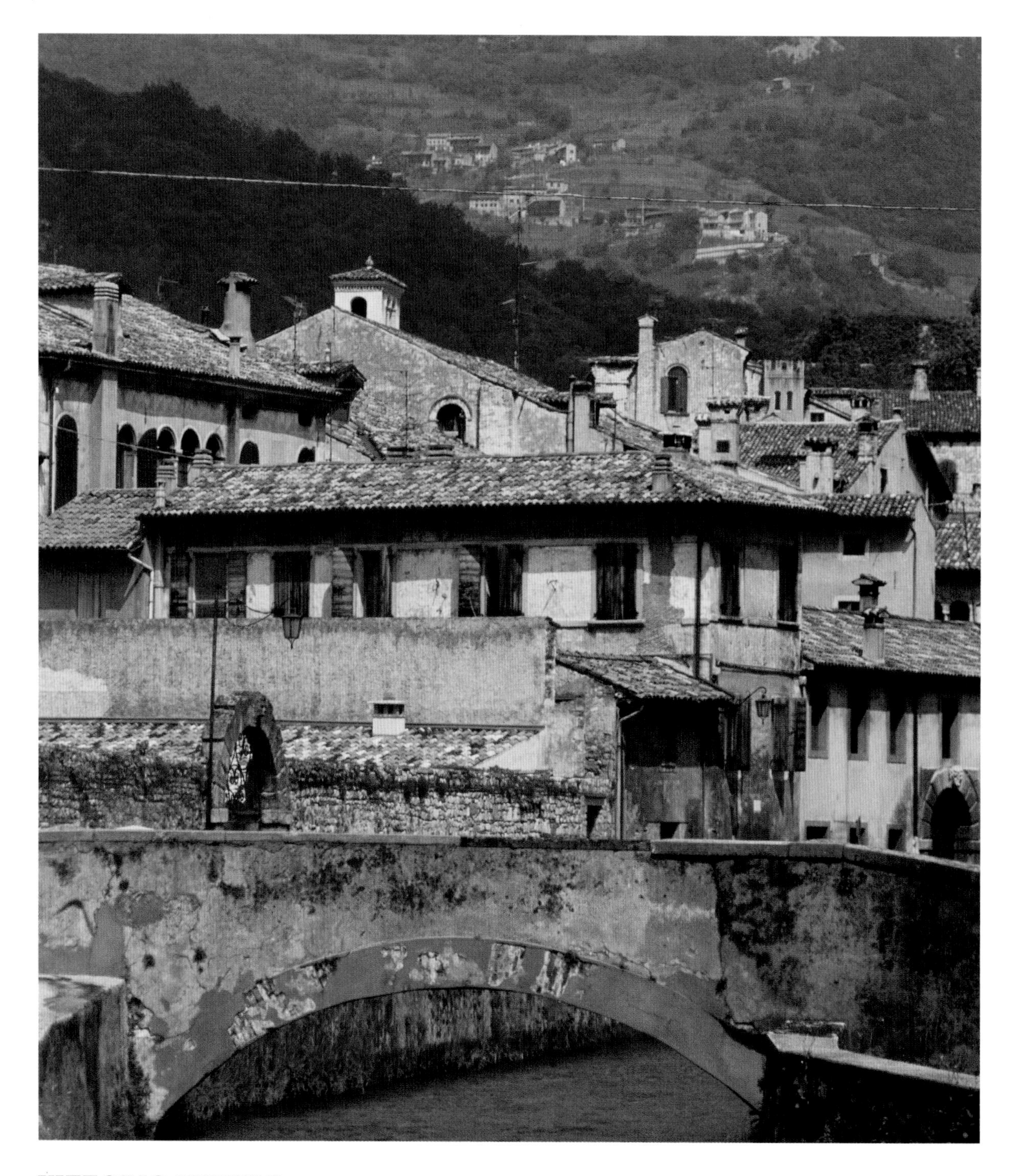

VITTORIO VENETO

(*above*)

Vittorio Veneto is actually an amalgamation of two towns—Cèneda and Serravalle—thrust together in 1866 to honor Italy's new king, Vittorio Emanuele. The river Meschio runs through the old town, which has managed to keep much of its charm despite being the site of the Italian army's last battle in World War I.

LAGO MISURINA

(*opposite*)

The crystal-clear waters of Lago Misurina reflect the surrounding snow-capped mountains, including the distinctive and dramatic Sorapiss, in shimmering colors. At 5,755 feet above sea level, and ringed by abundant forest, Misurina's air is as clear as her waters, making the lake one of the unforgettable panoramas of Northern Italy.

PADUA'S DUOMO

(*below*)

A church has existed on the site of Padua's Duomo since 313 AD. The first was rebuilt after an earthquake in 1117, and the current edifice (the third) was begun in 1552. It was not completed until 1754, and to this day the facade remains unfinished. The interior, though, is an impressive, calm space amid a bustling modern city.

BASILICA DI SANT'ANTONIO, PADUA

(*opposite*)

Donatello's statue of the mercenary soldier Gattamelata, the first large bronze sculpture of the Renaissance, stands guard over St Anthony of Padua, whose remains are enshrined in this unusual church. The basilica was built over many years, starting in 1232, and its lavish domes, gables and belfries reflect a variety of architectural styles.

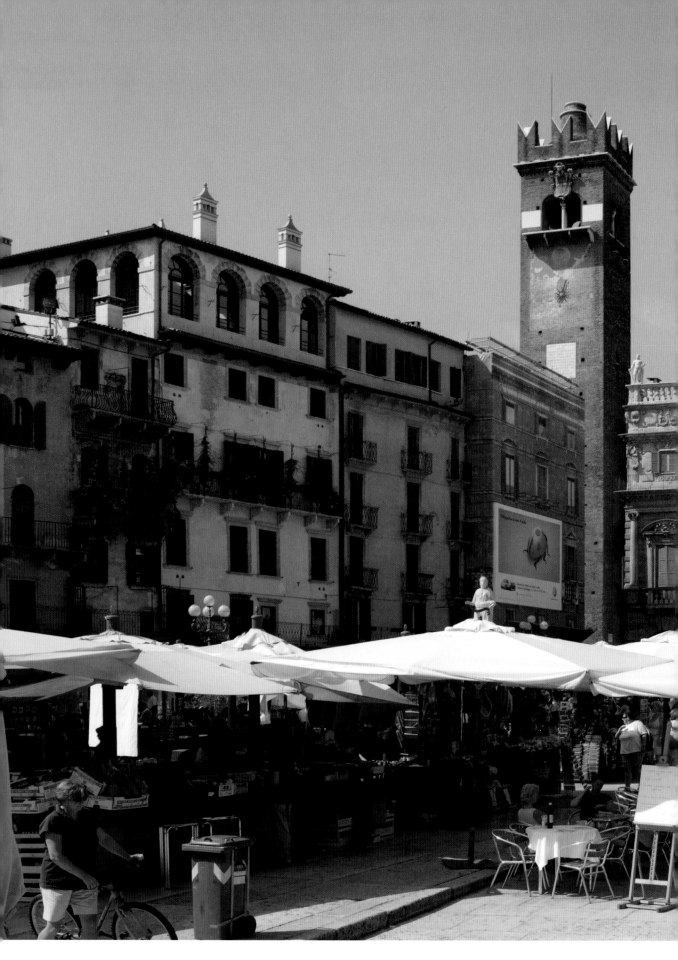

PIAZZA DELLE ERBE, VERONA

(previous pages)

The heart of the city since the days of the Roman Empire, the lively Piazza delle Erbe is filled with cafés and stalls and is enclosed by elegant palazzi. The name comes from the city's old herb market, but today's stalls trade in all sorts of culinary delights, from suckling pig to wild mushrooms.

VERONA

(below)

From the spectacular vantage point of the Museo Archeologico, the River Adige—flanked by pink-hued medieval buildings and magnificent Roman landmarks—meanders through the irresistible city of Verona. The characteristic pink tinge of her fine palazzi comes from the *rosso di Verona*—the local reddish limestone, preferred by the city's medieval rulers.

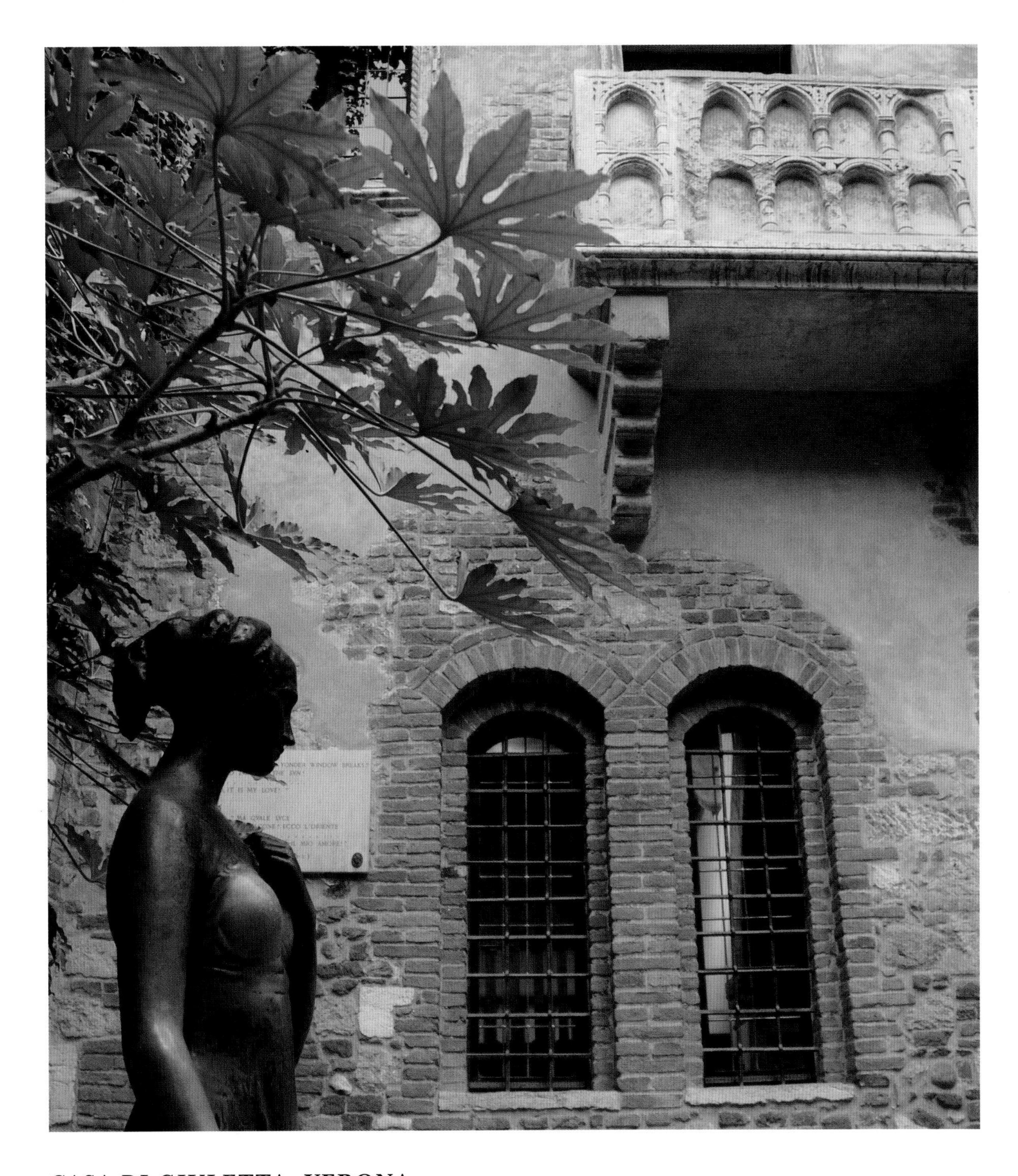

CASA DI GIULETTA, VERONA
(*above*)

The story of the star-crossed lovers Romeo and Juliet written by Luigi da Porto of Vicenza in the 1520s and made famous by William Shakespeare, has inspired countless dramas, ballets, and films. Lovers young and old flock to recreate the most famous scene from *Romeo and Juliet* from the balcony of this fine fourteenth-century house at 23 Via Cappello.

SAN GIORGIO MAGGIORE, VENICE

Separated from the main body of Venice by St. Mark's Basin, the island of San Giorgio Maggiore retains a quiet, meditative air. The classic Renaissance basilica, designed by the influential sixteenth-century architect Andrea Palladio, is the focal point from all directions and one of the most prominent Venetian landmarks.

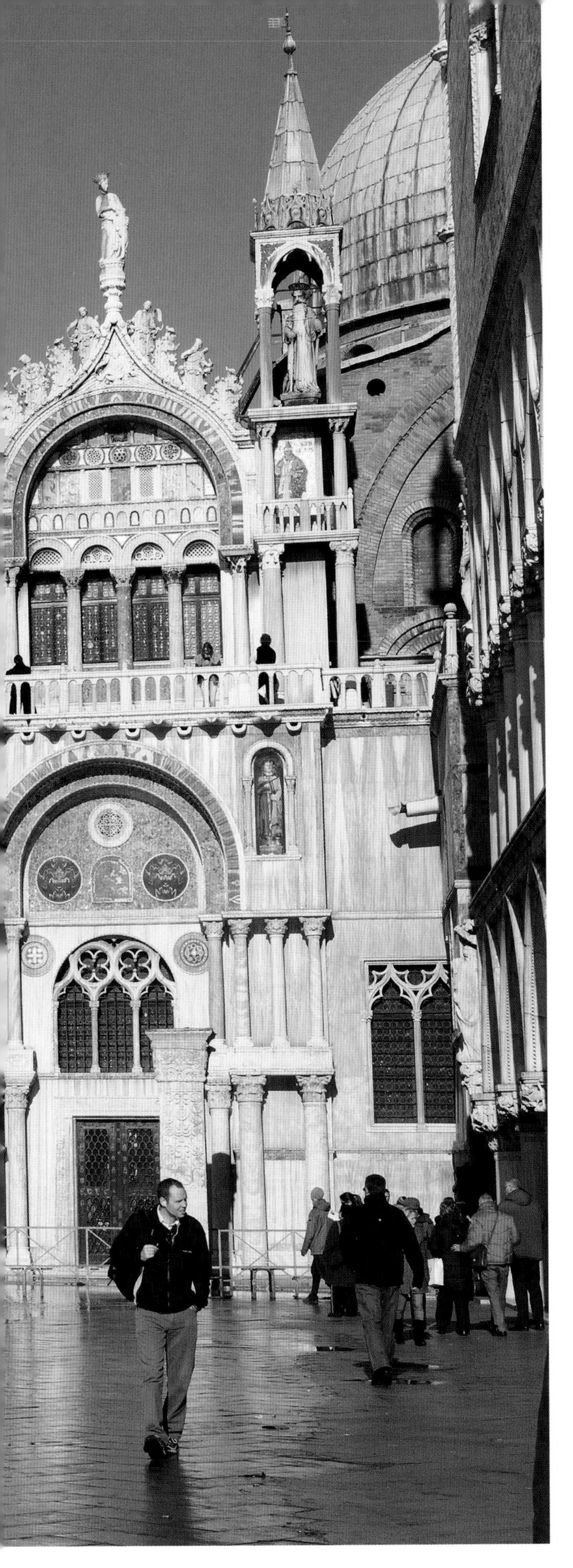

BASILICA DI SAN MARCO, VENICE

This breathtaking Byzantine basilica dominates the eastern end of the Piazza San Marco. Its ornate design was intended both as a symbol of the Venetian Republic's power, and to be a fitting resting place for the body of St. Mark. The western facade, facing onto the piazza, is a succession of domes, colums, arches, spires, marble statues, and glittering mosaics.

RIVA DEGLI SCHIAVONI, VENICE

(following pages)

Though thronged with tourists and souvenir stalls, the Riva degli Schiavoni offers a lovely promenade along the bank of St Mark's Basin, close to St Mark's Square. Many former palaces along the Riva have now been converted into glamorous hotels, including the fifteenth-century Hotel Danieli, with its pink Gothic facade.

DANIELI EXCELSIOR

DANIELI

RIO DELLA PAGLIA, VENICE
(*opposite*)

The graceful design of the gondola, that quintessential image of Venice, has changed little since the end of the seventeenth century. The elaborately carved oarlock—the *forcola*—allows the skilful gondoliers to negotiate the city's narrowest canals and lowest bridges with ease.

RIALTO BRIDGE, VENICE
(*above*)

Completed in 1591, this most famous Venetian bridge was the first pedestrian walkway across the Grand Canal. A hotly contested competition for its design—in which eminent architects, including Michelangelo, Sansovino, and Palladio, all took part—was finally won by Antonio da Ponte, whose audacious plans took three years to realize.

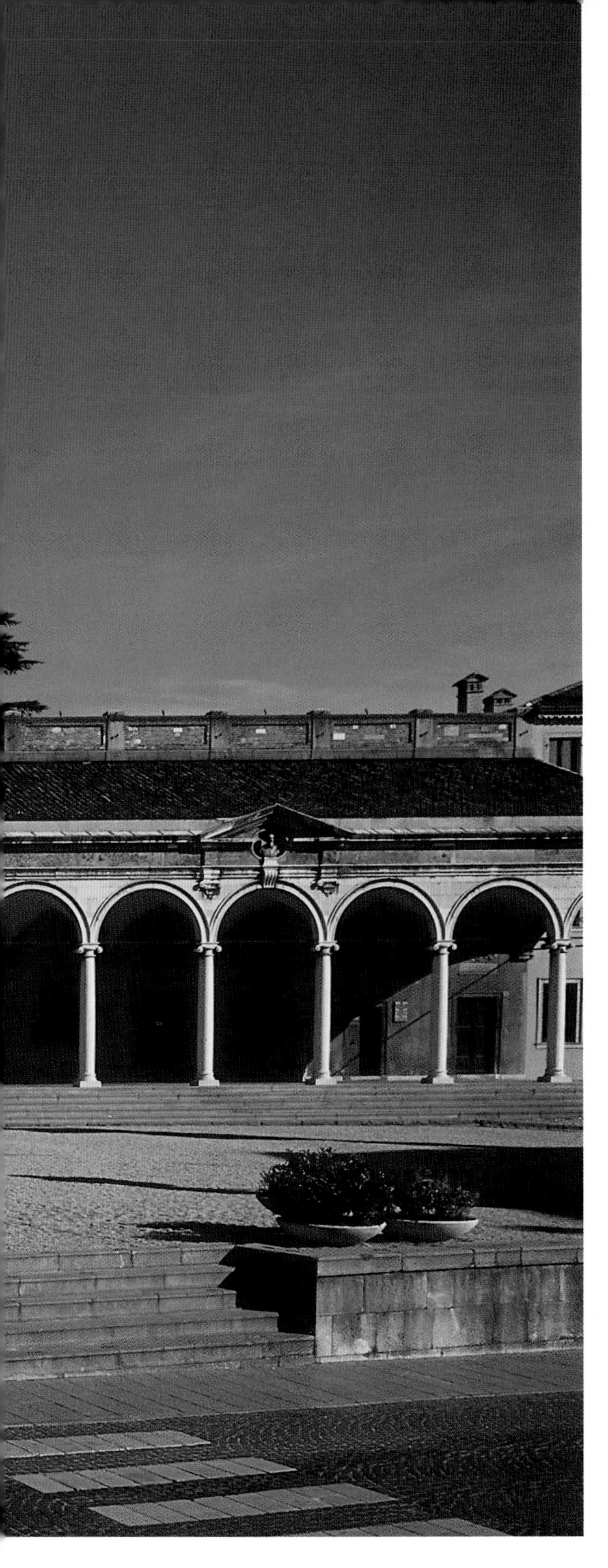

PORTICATO DI SAN GIOVANNI, UDINE

Udine's central Piazza della Libertà is dominated by this impressive Renaissance colonnade, designed by Bernardino da Morcote in 1533. The clock tower was inspired by the blue-and-gold face of its counterpart in Venice's St. Mark's Square and, like that famous structure, is crowned by two bronze Moors who strike the hours.

NORTHERN ITALY

Lombardy & The Lakes

The awe-inspiring natural beauty of the Italian Lakes is something no visitor to the region could ever forget. Lakes Como, Maggiore, and Garda feature high on the list of Italy's most romantic destinations, as charming villages and splendid waterside villas look out over unrivaled mountain scenery. The region, especially the stylish capital Milan, is an economic powerhouse, but tourists flock to the city for its stunning Gothic cathedral (and perhaps the shopping). Smaller settlements, such as medieval Pavia and Bergamo, and Mantua with its Renaissance splendors, are reminders of a time when local rulers supported the very finest art and architecture. Spectacular religious edifices and remnants of ancient Roman rule are apparent throughout the region, in towns such as historic Brescia and in the imposing monastery of Certosa di Pavia.

VILLA DEL BALBIANELLO, LAKE COMO

Built in 1787 on the site of a Franciscan Monastery, the spectacular vistas and elaborate terrace gardens of the Villa del Balbianello may be familiar as sets from films such as *Star Wars Episode II: Attack of the Clones* (2002) and *Casino Royale* (2006).

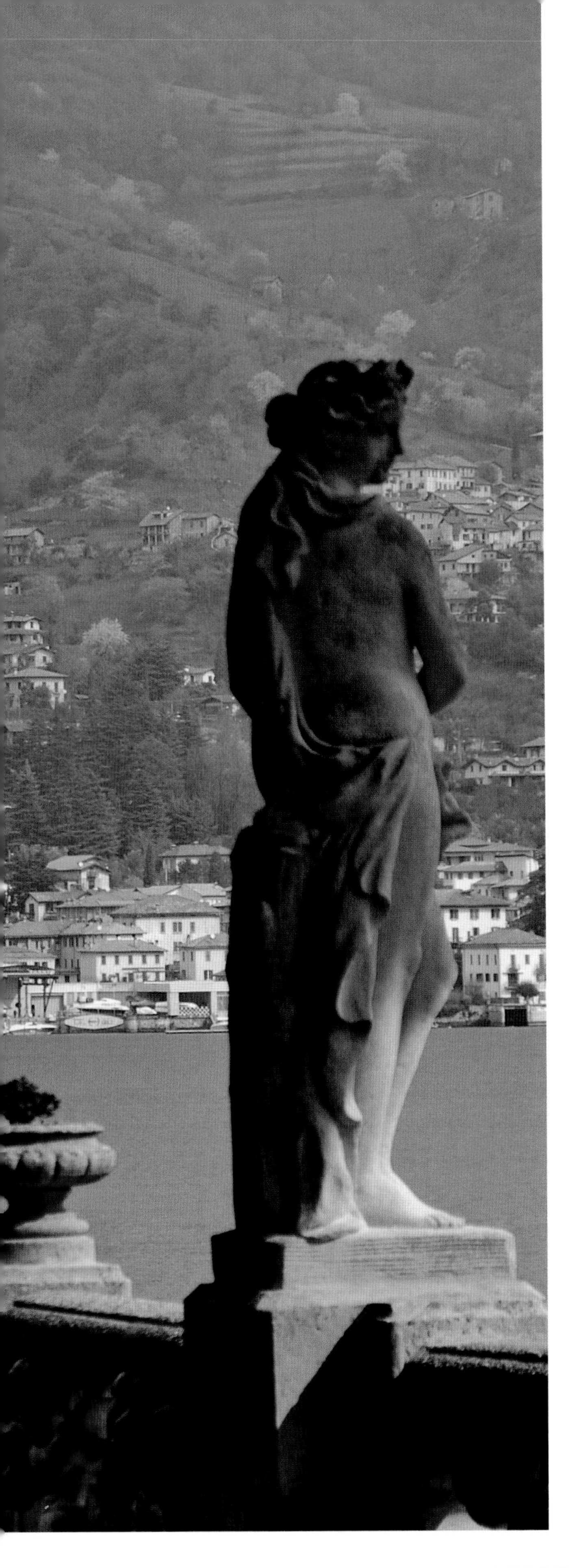

VIEW FROM THE LOGGIA OF VILLA DEL BALBIANELLO

(opposite)

Villa Balbianello, situated at the tip of a wooded peninsula on the southwest branch of Lake Como, enjoys unimpeded views of the surrounding hills and the nearby town of Lenno. After centuries in private hands, the Villa is now owned by the Fondo Ambiente Italiano, ensuring that the general public can now enjoy this spectacular setting.

SANTA CATERINA DEL SASSO, LAKE MAGGIORE

(following pages)

Nestled into the cliffs on the shore of Lake Maggiore—and visible only from the water—this beautiful, tiny, stone monastery was built to honor St. Catherine of Alexandria in 1170. A local sailor caught in a storm invoked the help of St. Catherine and survived; the cave in which he sought shelter became a votive chapel, which grew over several centuries into this small complex of buildings.

ISOLA BELLA, LAKE MAGGIORE

(*opposite*)

Once a small fishing village, this island was gradually transformed into the grand home of the wealthy Borromeo family. Carlo III Borromeo began the extensive upgrade of this modest rock in 1630, importing soil, fountains, statues, white peacocks, and a host of shrubbery and trees, and building an opulent *palazzo*. This vast project took over 60 years to complete, but the results, as well as the setting, are truly breathtaking.

ISOLA MADRE, LAKE MAGGIORE

(*below*)

Also owned by the Borromeo family, Isola Madre is larger and less ostentatious than Isola Bella. It is famed for its beautiful botanic gardens, which have a lusher, wilder feel than the neatly tended terracess of her neighbour to the south. Visitors come to see the azaleas, hibiscus, wisteria, and Kashmir cypress, as well as the pretty *palazzo*.

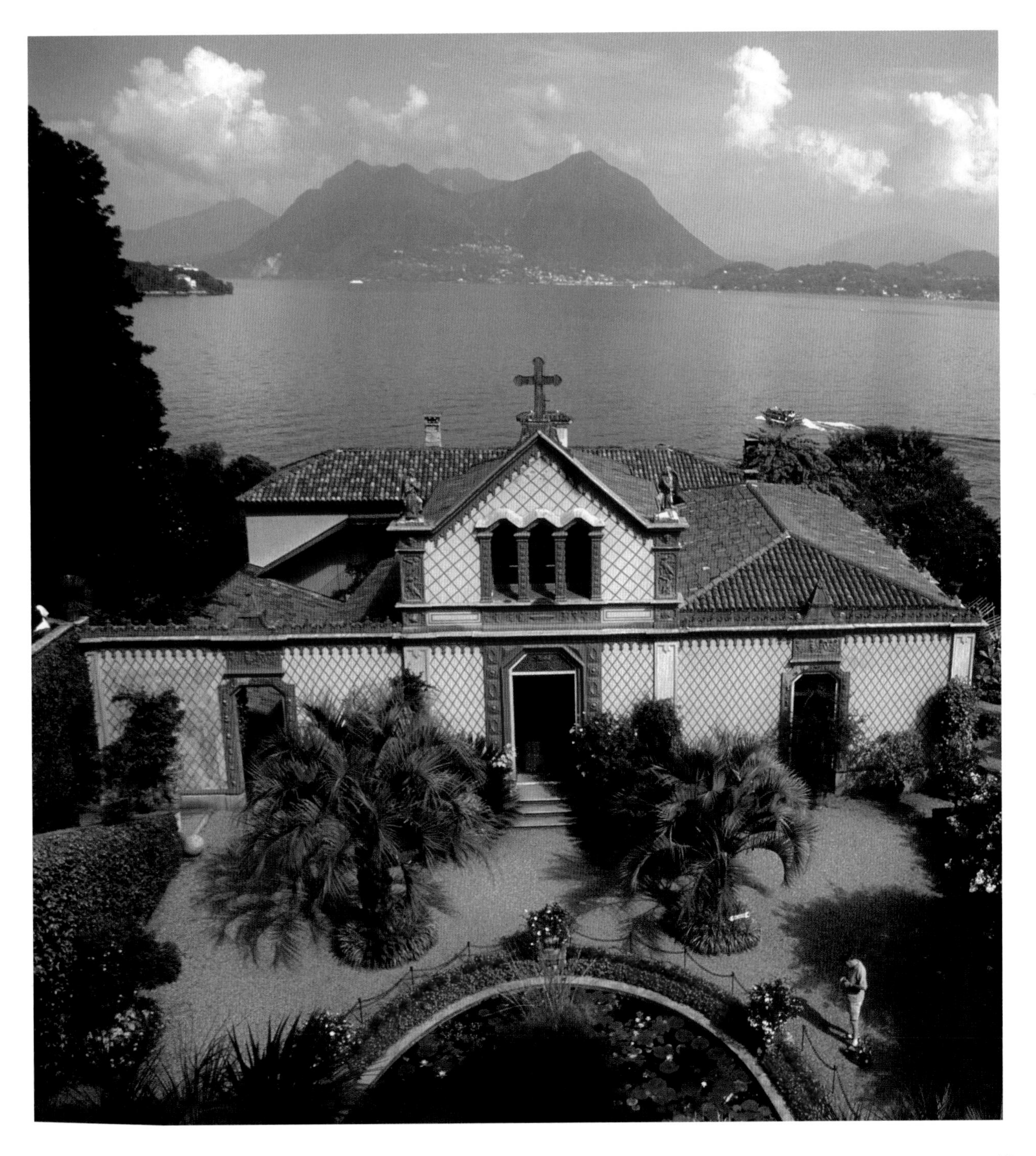

DUOMO FACADE, MILAN

(*below*)

Milan's giant Duomo is one of the largest Gothic churches in the world, and took over 500 years to complete—hardly surprising when you consider the exquisite, elaborate work that has gone into every single feature. In this detail of the facade, Christ is surrounded by his persecutors.

DUOMO ROOF, MILAN

(*opposite*)

The roof is another spectacular feature of Milan's Duomo—no fewer than 135 spires pierce the skyline, amid innumerable statues and gargoyles. Visitors come not only to see the ornate craftsmanship, but also to admire the wonderful views across the city and as far as the Alps.

PALAZZO TE, MANTUA

(opposite)

This fantasy palace in the suburbs of Mantua was designed by Giulio Romano in the 1520s for Duke Federico Gonzago and his mistress, as a base for entertaining and hunting. It is lavishly decorated with ornate frescoes and paintings, many of which were executed by Romano himself. Those opposite are from the ceiling of the *Sala dei Venti* (Room of the Winds) and depict mythological and zodiacal figures.

CERTOSA DI PAVIA

(right)

This magnificent Carthusian monastery complex, five miles north of the medieval town of Pavia, is the pinnacle of Renaissance architecture in Lombardy. Founded by the Duke of Milan in 1396 and greatly expanded in the fifteenth century, its design was the responsibility of successive generations of the Solari family of architects. Though it was declared a national monument in 1866, the monastery is still occupied by a small group of Cistercian monks.

DUOMO VECCHIO, BRESCIA

(opposite)

Brescia's striking old cathedral, also known as *La Rotonda*, is a unique circular church of local stone, dating from the twelfth century. Inside a glass floor reveals remains of Roman baths and the apse of an eighth-century basilica, destroyed by fire in 1097.

LAKE GARDA

(following pages)

Surrounded by mountains and with scenic little villages dotting its edges, Italy's largest lake (at 31 miles in length), and its most visited, is always alluring. The view here is from the popular resort of Riva del Garda, which is a great base for sailing and other watersports. The town also boasts a charming piazza and pedestrianized old quarter.

NORTHERN ITALY

Piemonte • Valle d'Aosta • Liguria

The northwestern extreme of Italy, Piemonte and Valle d'Aosta, borders the French and Swiss Alps. It is a region of valleys and mountains, perfect terrain for a major wine industry. Although an industrial city, Turin boasts an appealing, historic Baroque center, while, farther south, Alba's cobbled streets and medieval towers are at the heart of a proud and vibrant community, renowned for its superb local produce. Mont Blanc dominates the far northwest of Valle d'Aosta, where spectacular views are afforded to the many visiting walkers and skiers. Curving around the coast, Liguria is home to the ancient port of Genoa, with its eclectic and varied architecture. The region also contains the Italian Riviera, with its popular sandy beaches, and one of Italy's most picturesque coastal destinations, the Cinque Terre, with its five delightfully colored villages dramatically situated on an appealing stretch of rugged coastline.

BASILICA DI SUPERGA, TURIN

A notable example of the Baroque architecture often found in the region, the pastel-shaded Basilica di Superga is located at the top of a hill overlooking Turin. The central dome tops out at an impressive 213 feet, and is flanked on either side by twin bell towers. The interior is equally magnificent, featuring numerous fine carvings and paintings.

VINUM FESTIVAL, ALBA

(previous pages)

Alba is a major producer of red wine—a bewildering array of Barolos and Nebbiolos are bottled in the surrounding hills. At the annual spring festival, locals in the town play a game of fishing for bottles of wine in celebration of this rich viticultural heritage.

ALPINE ROAD, VALLE D'AOSTA

(below)

In the semi-autonomous and sparsely populated region of Valle d'Aosta, a herd of cattle are driven along the picturesque winding road from the ski resort town of La Thuile towards the Col de l'Iseran on the French border, the highest paved mountain pass in the Alps.

MONT BLANC

(following pages)

Climbers view the top of Mont Blanc (Monte Bianco in Italian), the highest mountain in Western Europe, above the town of Courmayeur close to the French border. Although not the most dangerous climb in the Alps, the Mont Blanc massif still claims around 100 lives each year.

GENOA

(previous pages)

Fronted by a natural harbor and backed by protective mountains, Genoa rose to prominence as a maritime power over the course of the sixteenth century, and remains Italy's most important commercial port. Her old city, home to the explorer of the Americas, Christopher Columbus, is a maze of narrow streets, *palazzi,* and churches.

CARRODANO, LA SPEZIA

(left)

Although it's usually the Cinque Terre and the beautiful coastline that draw people to the province of La Spezia, traveling inland reveals wide valleys, wooded hills, vineyards, and picturesque villages—such as Carrodano—that are well worth exploring.

SAN REMO BEACH

(below)

The classiest of the Italian Riviera's beach resorts benefits from a mountain backdrop and a reputation for attracting the rich and famous—Alfred Nobel and Pyotr Tchaikovsky both stayed here, in the stuccoed mansions of the palm-lined seafront avenue. The old town is a charming huddle of narrow lanes, medieval houses, and pastel-colored shutters.

MANAROLA, CINQUE TERRE

(following pages)

The folded stretch of coast known as the Cinque Terre is the scenic highlight of the Italian Riviera. Manarola, probably the oldest of the five tiny villages that give the region its name, is remarkable for the breathtaking beauty of its situation with clusters of colorful houses clinging precariously to a rugged shore surrounded by sea.

NORTHERN ITALY

Emilia-Romagna

Superbly preserved medieval hill towns, such as Castell'Arquato, are one of this region's many attractions. An array of castles in the vicinity of Parma, including Torrechiara, also stand out in a variety of beguiling rural landscapes, a picturesque reminder of medieval and Renaissance days when local nobility built superb fortresses and palaces and literally held court. The cities of Bologna (long a home for both learning and gastronomy) and Ferrara (a center of Renaissance heritage) compete for attention with Ravenna, once the capital of the Western Roman empire. Each city offers a unique set of religious architectural styles and historical monuments to admire. South of the flatter countryside of Emilia-Romagna, from where much of the region's famous culinary produce orginates, are the atmospheric wetlands of the Po Delta, an area best explored by boat and famous for the diversity of its birdlife.

CATTEDRALE DI SAN GIORGIO, FERRARA

The stunning facade of the basilica of San Giorgio in Ferrara mixes Romanesque and Gothic styles. At its centre is a grandiose portal, begun in the twelfth century, with a carving of St. George and the Dragon above the doorway. On either side, the entrance columns are supported by telamons (shapes in the form of a man, also called an Atlas) sitting atop two stone lions.

CASTELLO ESTENSE, FERRARA

(*opposite*)

The formidable Castello that dominates Ferrara was built as a fourteenth-century moated fortress to protect the Este family from local uprisings. By the Renaissance it had been refashioned and expanded to become a sumptuous courtly residence. Its thick walls still conceal a few remnants of Ferrara's artistic flowering, which reached its height in the sixteenth century.

STATUE OF NICCOLÒ III D'ESTE, FERRARA

(*below*)

The Este nobility (including Niccolò III Marquis of Ferrara, whose equestrian statue adorns the facade of the Palazzo Municipale), was a major political force in Renaissance days. They were the patrons not only of major poets like Ariosto and Tasso, but also of artists and architects who, over the centuries, helped create a stylish urban center.

CASTELLO DI TORRECHIARA, PARMA

(*previous pages*)

Medieval castles are a major feature of the countryside around Parma. One of the best situated is Torrechiara some eleven miles south of Parma, which commands superb views of the area. It was built between 1448 and 1460 and includes frescoes by Bembo in the castle's celebrated gold room.

CASTELL'ARQUATO

(*below*)

At the center of this stunningly preserved and restored medieval town is the Piazza del Municipio. The town's prominence is owed to its lofty situation on a rock overlooking routes between Parma and Piacenza, though its historic center has not expanded much from Roman times when it was believed to have been a minor garrison.

PONTE VECCHIO, BOBBIO

(*opposite*)

One of the glories of the small town of Bobbio in the province of Piacenza is its bridge crossing the Trebbia river. Eleven irregular arches span the banks, hence its popular name of Ponte Gobbo (hunchback bridge). It dates back to the twelfth century, and there may have been a bridge on the same site in Roman times.

DUE TORRI, BOLOGNA
(*opposite*)

Bologna's famous "two towers" are the most prominent of what may have been as many as two hundred such structures across the city. The Torre Asinelli is 320 feet tall and offers superb views of Bologna, whereas the smaller Torre Garisenda leans heavily away from the perpendicular, having being shortened only a few years after completion to save it from collapse.

BOLOGNA AERIAL VIEW
(*facing page*)

Bologna's city center is famous for its covered walkways, or porticos, which from the thirteenth century have provided shelter from showers, and shade on hot summer days. Prominent in the picture is the city's cathederal, the Metropolitana di San Pietro, whose structure mostly dates from the seventeenth century.

BASILICA DI SAN VITALE, RAVENNA (*following pages*)

This remarkable church is a justly celebrated World Heritage Site that dates from the time when Ravenna was under the control of the Goths before an army of the Byzantine Emperor Justinian liberated the city. San Vitale was completed shortly after in 548 and contains some of the finest surviving examples of Byzantine mosaics. Those on the right represent two scenes from the life of Abraham: the first shows three angels announcing the birth of his son Isaac; the second depicts Abraham about to sacrifice his son.

MOSE
IEREMIA

RIVER PO, FERRARA
(opposite)

East of the city of Ferrara, the River Po divides into the channels of the Delta. This atmospheric, often misty, expanse of marshland, farmland, and lagoons grows a little each year and is the setting for one of Europe's most renowned centers for birdwatching.

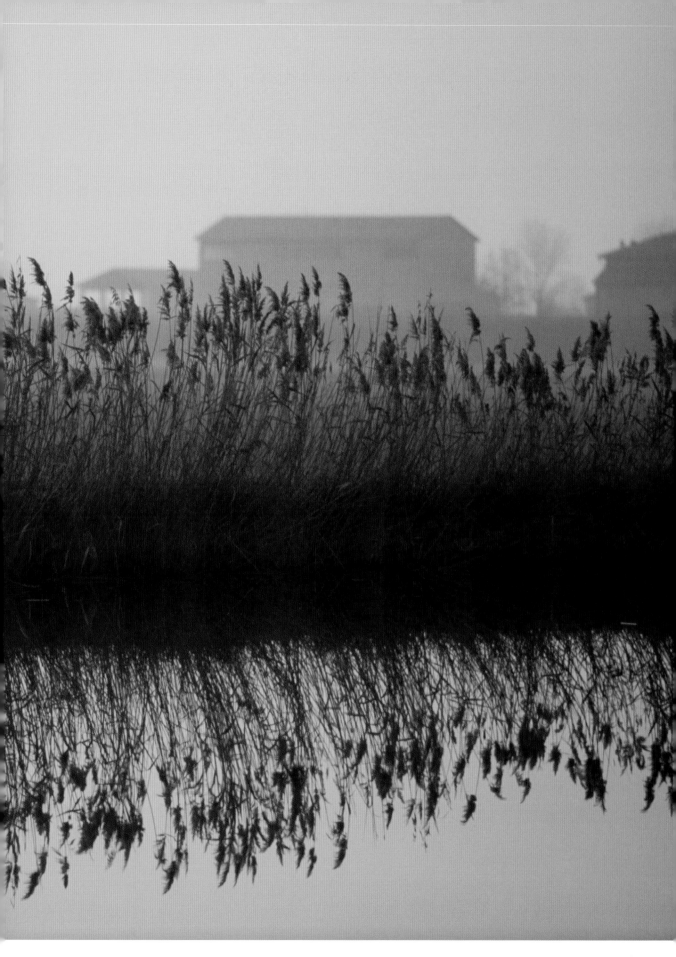

YHS

Central Italy

Le Marche • Abruzzo • Molise
Tuscany
Umbria
Rome • Lazio

CENTRAL ITALY

Le Marche ❧ *Abruzzo* ❧ *Molise*

Ihe three regions of Le Marche, Abruzzo, and Molise adjoin each other on the eastern coast of taly, marking the transition from north to south nd east to west. All three are sparsely populated nountain areas. In the north the beautiful hilltown of Urbino is famed for its Renaissance heritage—n particular the splendid Palazzo Ducale—while ts university helps provide the town with a lively ouzz. Further north the fortress of San Leo affords pectacular views of the mountains, while closer to he coast the well-preserved castle town of Gradara, vith its pinkish hues and fairy-tale battlements, s no less spectacular. The Majello National Park n Abruzzo (named for Mount Majello) provides tunning mountain scenery and wildlife but is ılso known for its many remote hermitages and nonasteries, such as the one at Corfinio. In Molise, Saepinum is a fascinating remnant of an old Roman orovincial town preserved remarkably intact due to ts isolated setting.

GRADARA

Crenellated medieval walls and mellow redbrick buildings urround the perfectly preserved castle at Gradara's summit, ınd give the town a fantasy atmosphere. The castle is notorious ıs the alleged scene of a thirteenth-century scandal involving Francesca da Rimini, who was married to Giovanni Malatesta out in love with his brother Paolo. Her jealous husband nurdered the two lovers and Dante famously immortalized heir story in Canto V of his *Inferno*.

CASTELLO DI SAN LEO

Clamped to the summit of a dizzying precipice, a fortress has existed at San Leo since the Romans founded a city on the rock. The current edifice dates from the fifteenth-century, but the area has always impressed visitors with its "harsh beauty"; in fact the poet Dante used it as the model for Purgatory in his *Divine Comedy.*

PALAZZO DUCALE, URBINO
(*opposite*)

In the mid-fifteenth century Federico da Montefeltro, the Lord of Urbino, established one of the most celebrated courts in all Europe—the inspiration for Castiglione's textbook of courtly behaviour, *The Book of the Courtier.* Federico's residence, the Palazzo Ducale, still dominates the city and commands fantastic views over the neighbouring countryside. It also contains one of the great collections of Renaissance paintings, the Galleria Nazionale delle Marche.

BASILICA DI SAN PELINO, CORFINIO

(*opposite*)

On the edge of the small village of Corfinio, in the beautiful surroundings of the Majella National Park, is the Basilica di San Pelino. There has been a church on the site since the fifth century AD but the current building dates from the twelfth century and is one of the finest Romanesque basilicas in Abruzzo. Adjacent to it is the Oratorio di Sant'Alessandro, one of several sites claiming to hold the bones of Pope Alexander I.

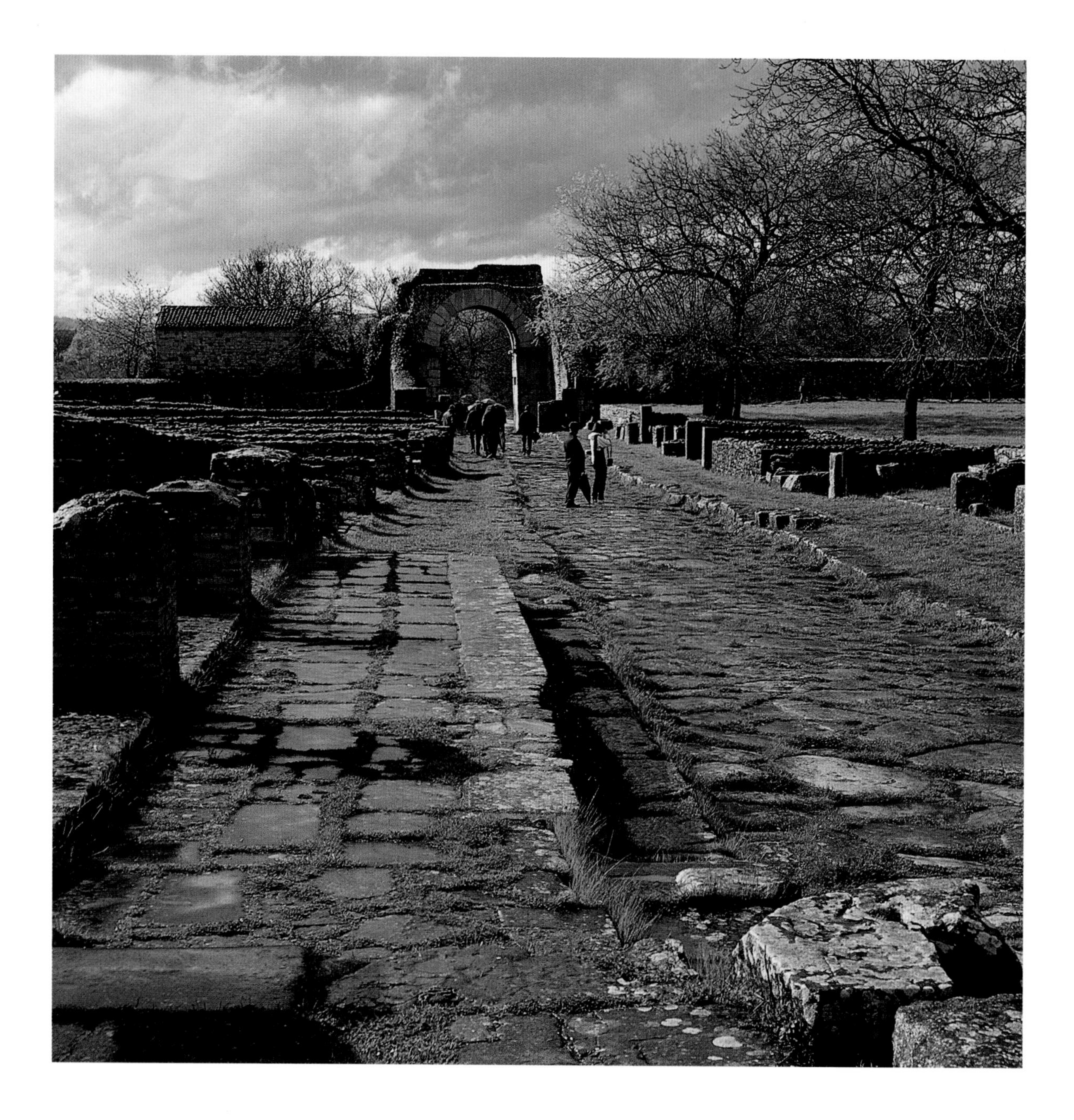

SAEPINUM

(*above*)

The Roman ruins of Saepinum are some of the best preserved in Italy, in part because they lie away from any of Molise's major cities.The town layout is based around four gates and two central avenues, the *decumanus maximus* and the north-south orientated *cardo maximus*. Saepinum is all the more charming for being surrounded by a scattering of farm buildings and cottages. The floor of the ancient forum is even used by local kids for soccer.

FRESCO, DUOMO DI ATRI

(*opposite*)

Atri is the prettiest in a series of small hill towns in Abruzzo—a warren of stepped streets, alleys, and passages. The Duomo, built on the site of a Roman bath, is worth visiting for Andrea Delitio's fifteenth-century fresco cycle, much of which focuses on the life of the Virgin Mary. Many of the scenes, such as *The Slaughter of the Innocents* and *The Virgin's Farewell to the Apostles*, have delightfully detailed architectural settings.

CENTRAL ITALY

Tuscany

Tuscany is the most quintessentially "Italian" of the country's regions. With its rural heartland dotted with cypresses, olive groves, and vineyards, this is a terrain that has changed little for centuries. In the middle ages the Tuscan dialect formed the basis of the Italian language and its major cities were at the heart of the most exciting developments in the ensuing Renaissance. Florence, in particular, boasts an extraordinary wealth of artistic riches, from sculpture by Michelangelo to the architectural masterpieces of Brunelleschi. Farther south, its archrival Siena hosts one of the great spectacles of Europe in the horse race known as the Palio, held in its vast central square, the Piazza del Campo. Pisa, with its incomparable LeaningTower, and the walled city of Lucca are scarcely less appealing, while the charming hill towns of San Gimignano and Montalcino epitomize a quieter charm. And if all this civilization gets to be too much, Elba's fine beaches are just a short boat trip away.

SANTA MARIA NOVELLA, FLORENCE

Built by the Dominicans between 1279 and 1357, the Gothic interior of Santa Maria Novella contains some superb frescoes, such as this example by Andrea di Bonaiuto in the Cappellone degli Spagnuoli (Spanish Chapel), showing demons mocking the souls in Limbo.

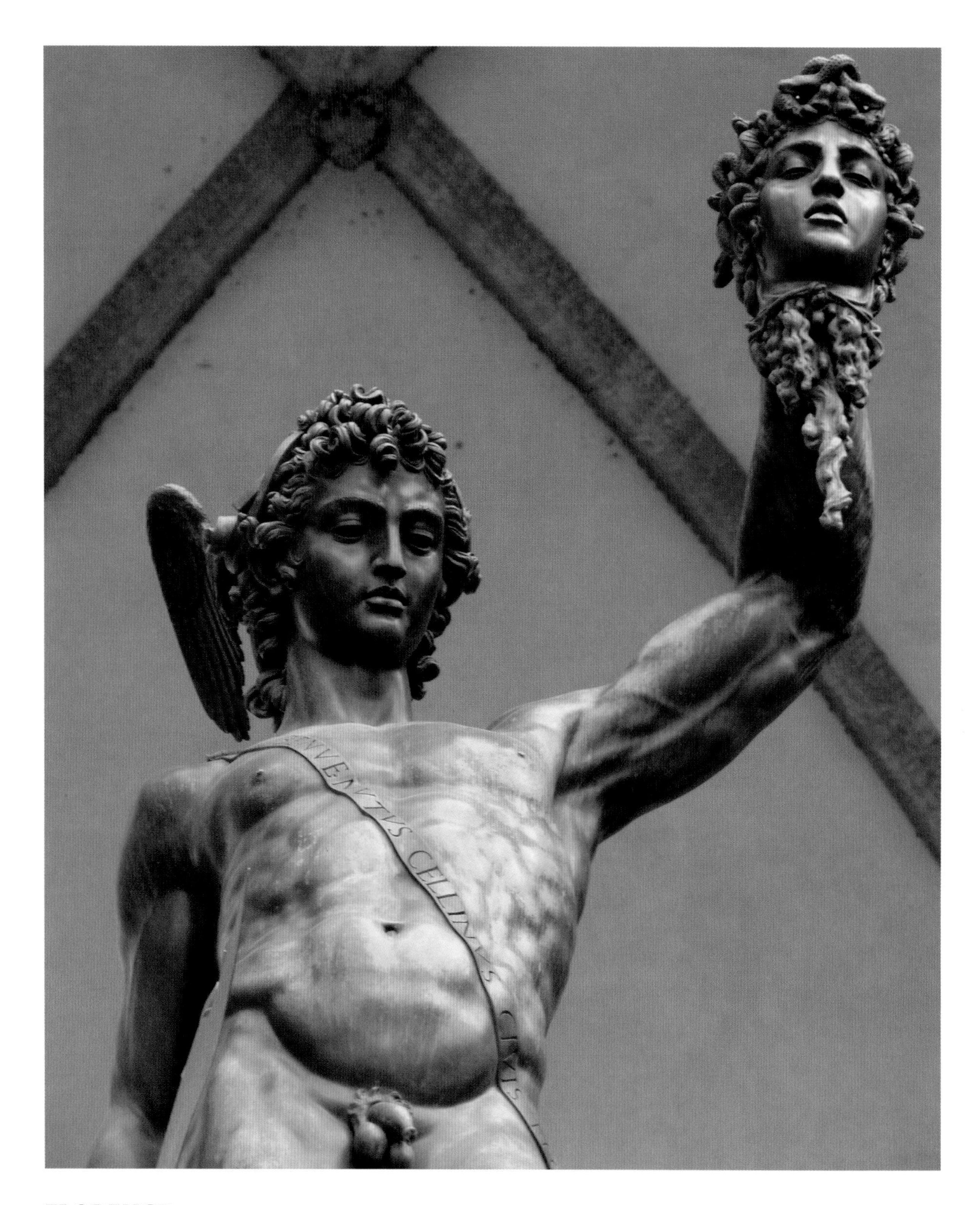

FLORENCE
(previous pages)

A panoramic view of Florence dominated by the fifteenth-century Duomo (left) and the Palazzo Vecchio (right). Situated on the River Arno and surrounded by hills, Florence is Tuscany's largest city and an irresistible magnet for lovers of Renaissance art.

LOGGIA DELLA SIGNORIA, FLORENCE
(above)

Bevenuto Cellini's bronze statue of *Perseus with the Head of Medusa* is located in the Loggia della Signoria, on the corner of the Piazza della Signoria. The Loggia is something of an open-air gallery that showcases numerous Roman and Mannerist sculptures.

PIAZZA DEL DUOMO, FLORENCE
(above)

The Duomo's striking multi-colored Gothic-style facade was actually a nineteenth-century addition. The design and construction of its huge masonry dome—a triumph of structural engineering—was masterminded by architect Filippo Brunelleschi and completed in 1469.

YHS
EX
DO

PIAZZA DELLA SIGNORIA, FLORENCE

(*opposite*)

The world's most famous statue is often said to be Michelangelo's *David*. The original stood for over 350 years on the Piazza outside the Palazzo Vecchio, a symbol of the freedom and independence of the city. By 1893 the weather had taken its toll and the statue was moved to the nearby Galleria dell'Accademia. David's imperious expression is said to be directed toward Rome.

MUSEO DEGLI ARGENTI, PALAZZO PITTI, FLORENCE

(*above*)

The vast and formidable Palazzo Pitti was originally built for banker Luca Pitti but soon became the base of the Medici dynasty. Today it contains several important museums, including the Museo degli Argenti (Silver Museum) which houses the Medici Treasury and is decorated with frescoes by Giovanni da San Giovanni celebrating the family's achievements.

FARMHOUSE, VAL D'ORCIA

This classic Tuscan view features a farmhouse surrounded by cypress trees in the World Heritage Site of Val D'Orcia, south of Siena. According to UNESCO, centuries of careful cultivation of the landscape following "an idealized model of good governance" have successfully created an "aesthetically pleasing picture." Tuscany's legendary beauty is not just opinion, but an official fact.

VILLA VIGNAMAGGIO, GREVE

(*above*)

The Villa Vignamaggio was once owned by the aristocratic Gherardini family and, according to legend, was the birthplace and summer residence of Lisa Gherardini, the supposed sitter for Leonardo da Vinci's *Mona Lisa*. The current villa, with its vast wine cellars, was built in the sixteenth century and is one of the oldest surviving estates in the Chianti Classico area. The setting for Kenneth Branagh's 1993 film *Much Do About Nothing*, it is now run partly as a hotel offering tours and wine tasting.

VILLA A SESTA, CHIANTI

(*opposite*)

Chianti wine is traditionally bottled in straw-covered rounded *fiaschi* (flasks), like those on this old vineyard cart. Tuscany's Chianti region lies between Florence and Siena and contains some of Italy's finest vineyards, including estates around the village of Villa a Sesta on the Castello di Brolio road. Meandering from vinyard to vinyard on a Chianti tasting tour is an essential Tuscan experience.

LEANING TOWER OF PISA

(opposite)

Even after the construction of a mere three stories in 1173, Pisa's most famous landmark began to veer from the perpendicular. Attempts to straighten the Leaning Tower (Torre Pendente) have been going on since it was completed in 1350, but the structure was only finally stabilized—at a safe five-degree angle—in 2001. A spiral staircase of 294 steps gets you to the bell chamber at the top the building, from where can you enjoy remarkable views across the city and beyond.

CAMPO DEI MIRACOLI, PISA

(above)

The area containing the Leaning Tower (far right), the Romanesque Duomo (centre) and the Baptistry (left) is known as the Campo dei Miracoli (Field of Miracles) because of the sheer magnificence of this trio of buildings. The fourth element (not visible here), is the Camposanto (Holy Field) which lies just to the north of the Duomo from where it appears as a vast screen of white marble. In fact this is just one side of a remarkable cloistered cemetery, built originally around soil brought from the Holy Land.

PONTE DELLA MADDALENA, LUCCA
(*above*)

This venerable pedestrian bridge across the River Serchio outside Lucca is named for Santa Maria Maddalena, but is more commonly known as the Ponte del Diavolo (the Devil's Bridge). According to legend the Devil agreed to complete the bridge for the official builder in exchange for the soul of whoever first walked across it. The builder kept his side of the bargain by sending a pig over the brand new bridge, much to the Devil's fury.

TORRE GUINIGI, LUCCA
(*opposite*)

This strange sight shows a group of holm oak trees planted on top of the Torre Guinigi, part of the fifteenth-century Casa Guinigi, home to a prosperous family of silk merchants. Such towers were built primarily as status symbols by wealthy citizens, and once dotted this elegant and charming town. Only nine of them still exist, including the nearby Torre delle Ore.

PORTOFERRAIO, ELBA
(*following pages*)

The island of Elba's coast is a major summer attraction with an excellent climate, unusually clear waters, white sand beaches, and a mountainous backdrop well adapted to walking. Portoferraio is its leading town, and is where Napoleon arrived in 1813 to take charge of the island under the terms of his enforced exile. Much of the island's early infrastructure dates from the dictator's period of rule.

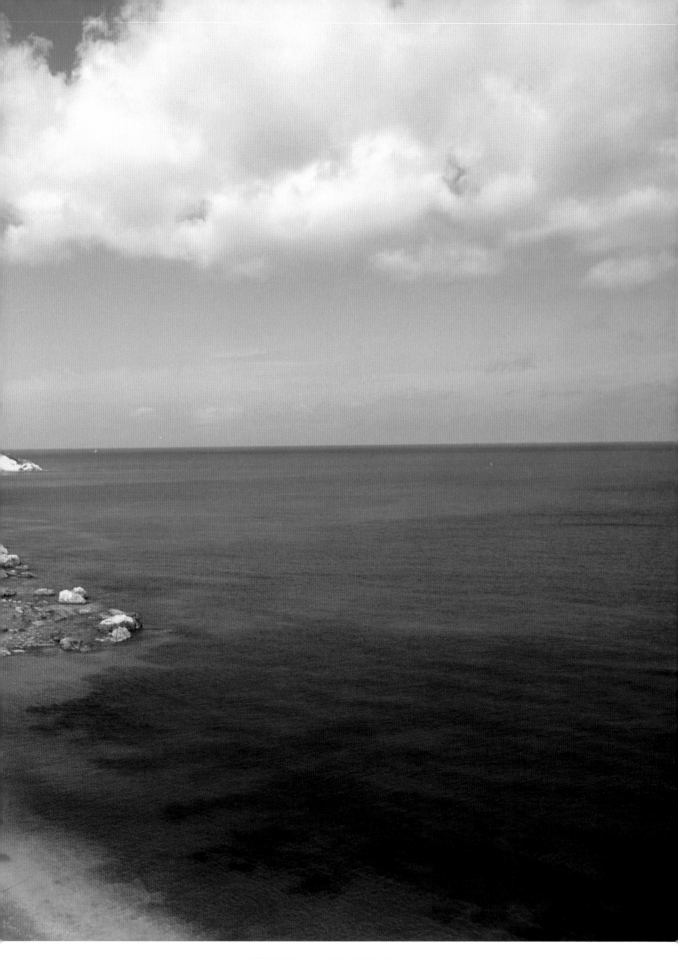

THE PALIO, SIENA

(*above*)

Italy's most thrilling festival consists of two horse races that take place between ten rival teams of *contrade* (districts) in Siena's Piazza del Campo. The event has been staged with very few changes since the thirteenth century with professional jockeys riding bareback on behalf of their *contrade.* The races, which take place on July 2 and August 16, are always fiercely contested with suspicions of Machiavellian intrigue and fixing.

CORTEO STORICO, SIENA

(*above*)

Two hours before the Palio gets underway there is a spectacular historical pageant, called the Corteo Storico, during which horses, riders, and *contrade* officials parade through the city's center accompanied by drummers, pages, and *sbandieratori* (heraldic flag-waving). With all those involved lavishly costumed, it is not difficult to imagine that you have been transported back in time.

PALAZZO PUBBLICO, PIAZZA DEL CAMPO, SIENA

(*opposite*)

Siena's medieval main square the Piazza del Campo, known simply as Il Campo, is the heart of Siena and one of the great civic spaces of Italy. Its red brick paving is divided into nine segments, a reference to the Council of Nine who governed the city in the fourteenth century. The Campo is dominated by the imposing Palazzo Pubblico (right) with its giant bell tower, the Torre del Magia, looming over the piazza.

SAN GIMIGNANO

(opposite)

Aristocratic rivalry of the twelfth and thirteenth centuries was the spur behind the 'medieval Manhattan' skyline of San Gimignano's numerous towers. Fifteen out of an original seventy two towers survive in a town which has become one of the most visited in Italy. San Gimignano is also blessed with many fine frescoes, including an outstanding cycle by Domenico Ghirlandaio at the Cappella di Santa Fina.

VOLTERRA

(following pages)

A picturesque hilltop town built on a plateau surrounded by volcanic hills, Volterra is one of the oldest Etruscan settlements and has one of Italy's most impressive archeological museums, the Museo Etrusco Guarnacci. There are also significant Roman remains, including a well-preserved theater and some nearby baths. Interest in the town was boosted by the success of Stephanie Meyers' *Twilight* novels, in which Volterra is the home of a coven of vampires, the Volturi.

PIAZZA GRANDE, MONTEPULCIANO

(*above*)

The highest of all Tuscan hill towns, Montepulciano is the perfect combination of bustling squares, shady alleyways and noble palazzi. The great Renaissance architect Antonio da Sangallo the Elder designed the town's gates and walls as well as the delightful nearby church of San Biagio.

ABBAZIA DI SANT'ANTIMO

(*opposite*)

The Romanesque Abbazia di Sant'Antimo, south of Montalcino, is one of Italy's finest, isolated within postcard-perfect scenery of wooded hills, olive groves, and Tuscan fields. These days it is cared for by a small group of monks, whose melodious plainsong can be heard several times a day.

CENTRAL ITALY

Umbria

The only one of the country's five land-locked regions without a foreign border, Umbria has a good claim to be called Italy's "green heart." Sparsely populated and unspoiled, it abounds in beautiful countryside, with pastoral vistas in the east contrasting with wilder countryside further south in the upland plain of the Piano Grande. The hill-towns of Assisi and Orvieto are justly famous as great religious centers, but there are plenty of less well-known places worth visiting, like the charming hill-towns of Trevi and Narni. Umbria has many unexpected delights to offer, such as the village of Castelluccio—the highest settlement in the Appenines—or the stupendous medieval aquaduct at Spoleto. Close to the region's capital Perugia is Lago Trasimeno, attracting visitors both for watersports and its scenery, and no traveller should miss out on Umbrian cuisine—arguably the best in Italy—with its famous black truffles a particular delight.

ASSISI

Early morning mist rises from Assisi, the spiritual home of Umbria and the birth and burial place of the inspirational religious figure Saint Francis. This view is from the Rocca Maggiore, a castle reached via the town's quietest streets up the steep slope from the basilica.

BASILICA DI SAN FRANCESCO, ASSISI

(opposite)

The Upper Church of the Basilica was built in honor of Saint Francis in the thirteenth century on a grander scale than might have been expected for an man who preached a gospel of humility and simplicity. A major destination for Catholic pilgrims, Assisi's five million visitors a year are also drawn here by the remarkable fresoces of Giotti and Pietro Lorenzetti.

ASSISI

(above)

Assisi town huddles on a low spur of Monte Subasio overlooking the famously flat Vale of Spoleto. When in the evening the coach parties have departed, the town retains a dignified and serene atmosphere. Though two devastating earthquakes shook the town in 1997, it has recovered well. The Basilica's foundations have been further strengthened in order to resist any seismic activity in the future.

PASSIGNANO, LAGO TRASIMENO

(following pages)

Trasimeno is Italy's fourth largest lake and highly popular with watersports enthusiasts, from windsurfers to speedboat owners. Boat trips can also be taken to Isola Maggiore and Isola Polvese, two of the lake's three islands. It's also worth checking out the local freshwater fish dishes at one of the numerous restaurants at Passignano or the nearby town of Castiglione del Lago.

DUOMO, ORVIETO
(*above*)

The facade of Orvieto's duomo features four enormous pillars that sustain a structure that is approximately 171 feet high high, which was completed over a period of three hundred years. The result: a harmonious exemplar of "transitional Romanesque-Gothic" and one of Umbria's biggest attractions. The interior contains masterly and influential frescoes by Luca Signorelli.

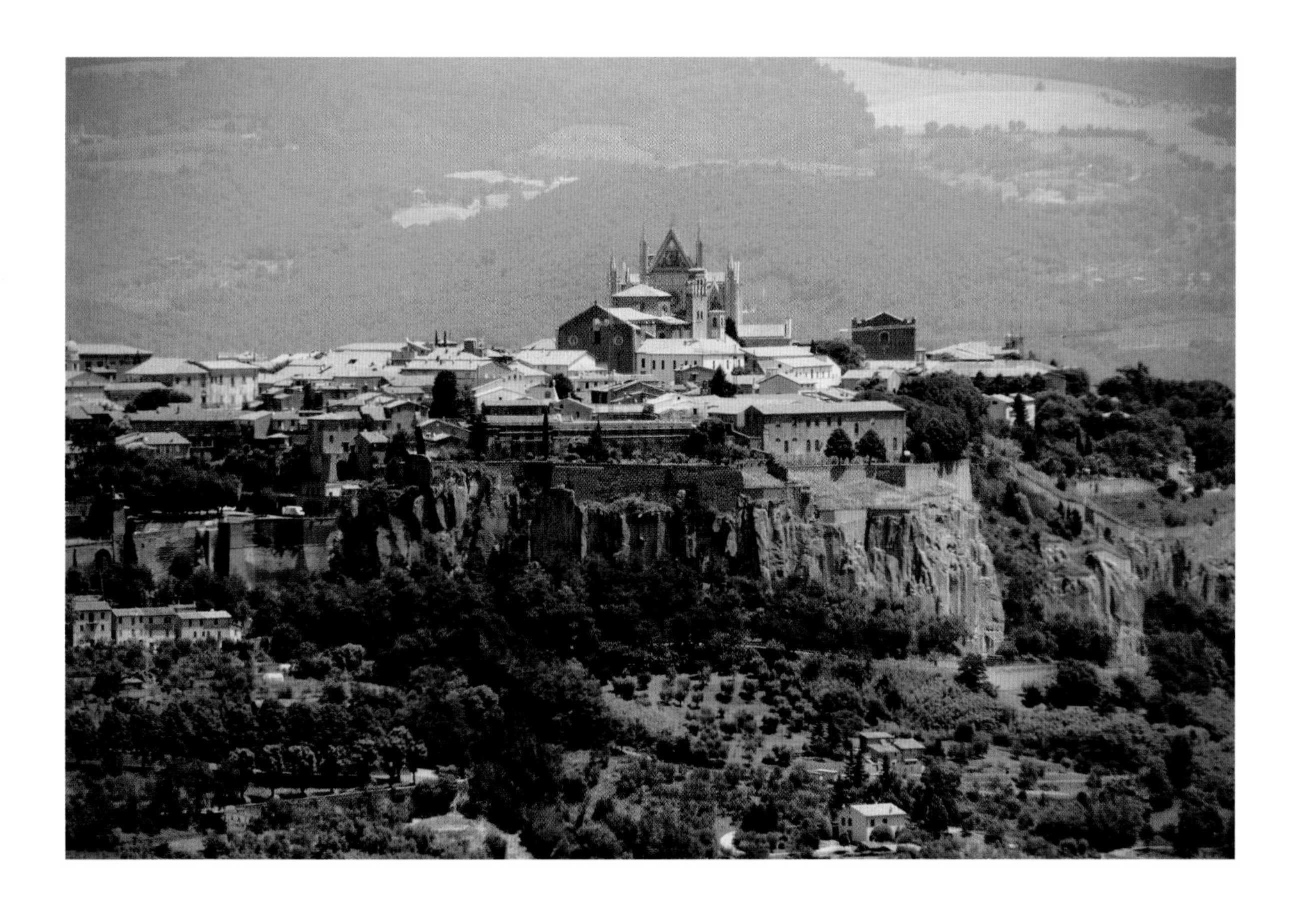

ORVIETO (*above*)

Situated in a strategic vantage point in the west of Umbria between Rome and Florence, Orvieto stands atop a foundation of volcanic rock. Below the sheer cliffs is a valley brimming with vineyards producing fine white wines made mainly from Grechetto and Trebbiano grapes. The towns cliffs house a network of caves that have been used since Etruscan times for a variety of purposes, and include a 118-foot well, the Pozzo della Cava, built as an enormous water store in 1530.

BAS RELIEFS, DUOMO, ORVIETO (*opposite*)

Lorenzo Maitani's graphic depiction of tormented souls being transported to Hell on Judgment Day are visible on a pillar of the Duomo's facade. On the four pillars many episodes from both the Old and New Testaments are carved with quite extraordinary detail and vividness.

NARNI

(*above*)

The medieval town of Narni in the wooded Nera valley is one of Umbria's most distinctive and unspoiled hill-towns in the south of Umbria close to the geographical center of the Italian peninsula. Below surrounded by trees lies the recently restored twelth-century Benedictine Abbazia di San Cassiano.

TREVI

(*opposite*)

Olive trees surround on all sides the unspoiled hill-town of Trevi. The town's eleventh-century Duomo San Emiliano occupies the highest vantage point. At the northern edge of Trevi is a former Franciscan convent, which is now home to the town's fascinating Museum of Olive Oil.

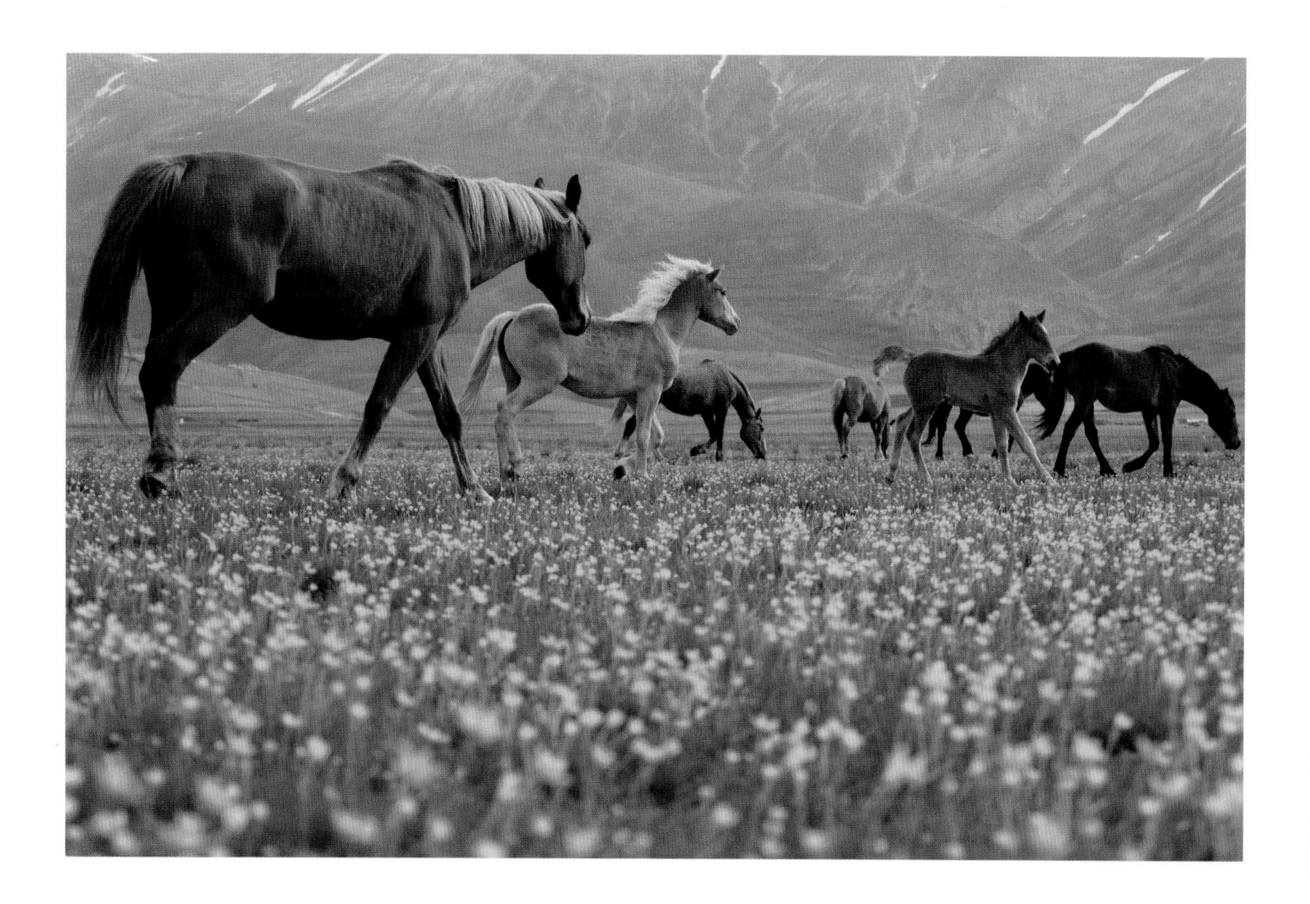

CASTELLUCCIO
(opposite)

The last of the day's sun catches the houses of the remote village of Castelluccio, set against the flank of Monte Vettore in the Sibillini mountain range. The farming village is 4,764 feet high and was originally a shepherds' community. Nowadays, outdoor activities such as hang gliding and tourism in summer, take the edge off Castelluccio's habitual isolation.

PIANO GRANDE DI CASTELLUCCIO
(above)

Spring and early summer, when a spectacular variety of wildflowers blooms, is the best time to visit the "great plain" on the eastern edge of Umbria. Wild horses can also occasionally be seen. The area is also renowned for a type of small and sweet brownish lentil, sold throughout Italy and regarded by connoisseurs as the best that money can buy.

PONTE DELLE TORRI, SPOLETO

Built on the foundations of a Roman aqueduct, the fourteenth-century Ponte delle Torri (Bridge of the Towers) is an awe-inspiring sight. Around 262 feet high with a span of 77 feet and ten arches, it seems to have been built to bring water from nearby Monteluco, but later formed part of the town's defenses. Today, you can walk across it and admire the wonderful view of the valley below.

CENTRAL ITALY

Rome ❧ *Lazio*

The hub of the vast Roman Empire and, after 1871, the capital city of a united Italy, Rome is one of the world's greatest cities, and has attracted hordes of fascinated sightseers since the eighteenth century. The city is literally monumental, boasting numerous well-preserved classical buildings—the Colosseum, the Forum, and the Pantheon—which epitomize the "grandeur that was Rome." It is also one of great centers of Christianity, with the head of the Catholic Church residing within his own mini-state, the Vatican—the site of the magnificent St Peter's Basilica. The Renaissance and Baroque eras saw the city transformed by the creations of visionary architects such as Bramante and Bernini. The region surrounding Rome, Lazio, offers its own share of memorable sights, such as the Villas at Tivoli and the fine ruins of ancient Ostia Antica. For lovers of the surreal, the startling Parco dei Mostri (Park of Monsters) at Bomarzo is an unforgettable experience.

THE COLOSSEUM

Rome's most recognizable marvel was originally called the Flavian Ampitheater. It was first completed in 80 AD with a maximum capacity at its peak of 70,000. Nearly two thousand years later, and despite a degree of wear and tear, it still retains the capacity to inspire.

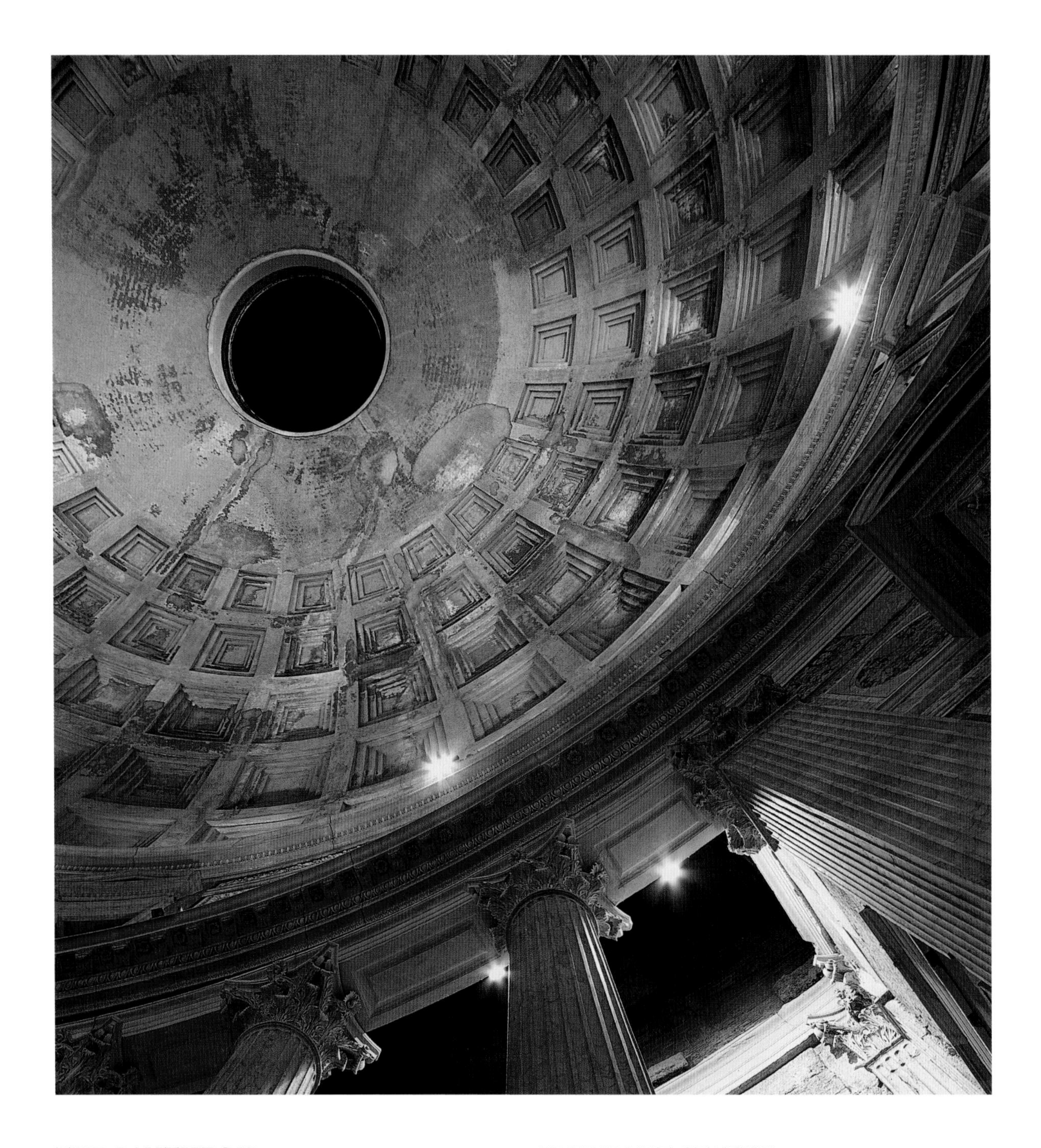

THE PANTHEON

(*above*)

The most intact of Rome's ancient structures and by dint of its harmonious proportions—the dome's diameter equals its height—one of the most impressive. The edifice was rebuilt by the Emperor Hadrian around 125 AD as a temple for all the gods—which is what *pantheon* means. The oculus (nearly thirty feet wide) in the center of the dome creates a magical 'spot' of sunlight which strikes the front entrance once a year at the summer equinox.

ELEPHANT STATUE

(*opposite*)

One of Rome's pleasures is seeing buildings of different periods in close and sometimes incongruous proximity. Here we see Baroque artist Gianlorenzo Bernini's statue of an elephant carrying an Egyptian obelisk on his back with the Pantheon visible behind. Out of vision nearby on the right is Rome's only Gothic church, Santa Maria Sopra Minerva, assembled on the ruins of a temple to the Roman goddess, Minerva.

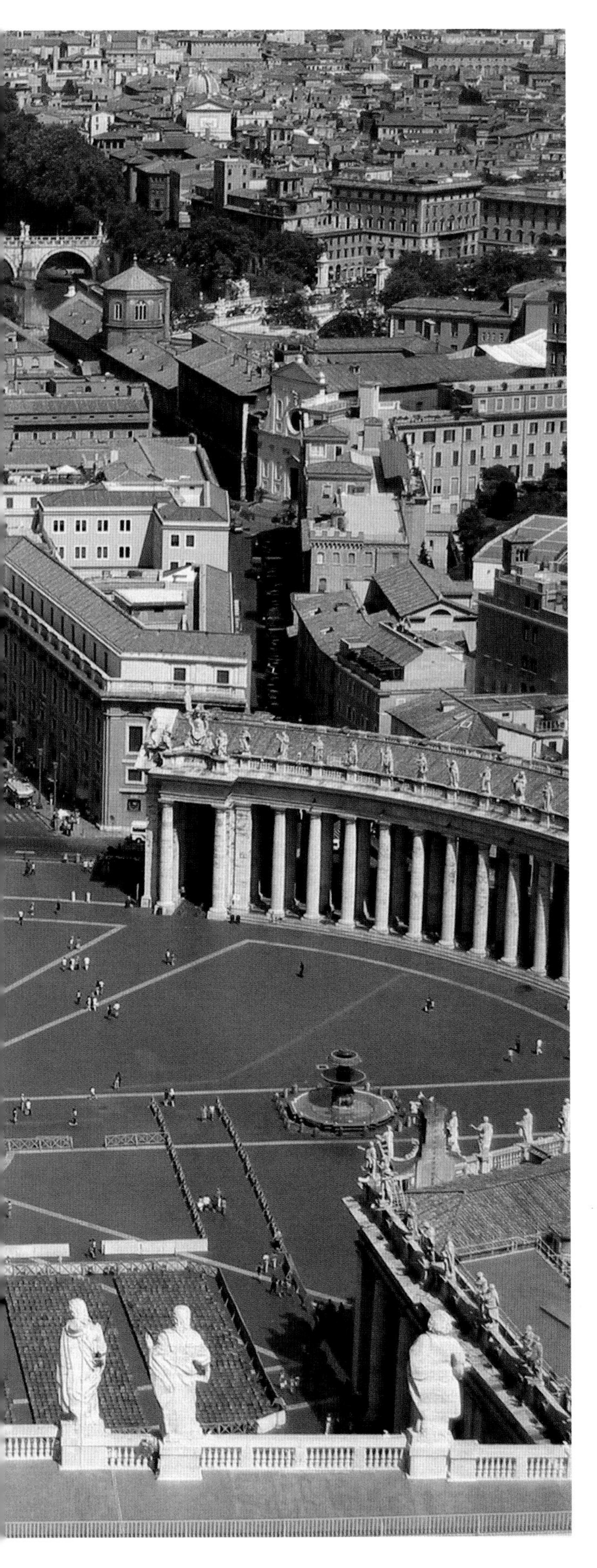

ST PETER'S SQUARE, VATICAN CITY

This view toward St. Peter's Square gives a good sense of the scale of the piazza. The Egyptian obelisk in the center of the picture was brought to Rome in 36 AD by the infamous Emperor Caligula and erected in its current position in 1586. The Vatican City has been a sovereign state since 1929; its thousand or so citizens and residents are presided over by the Pope.

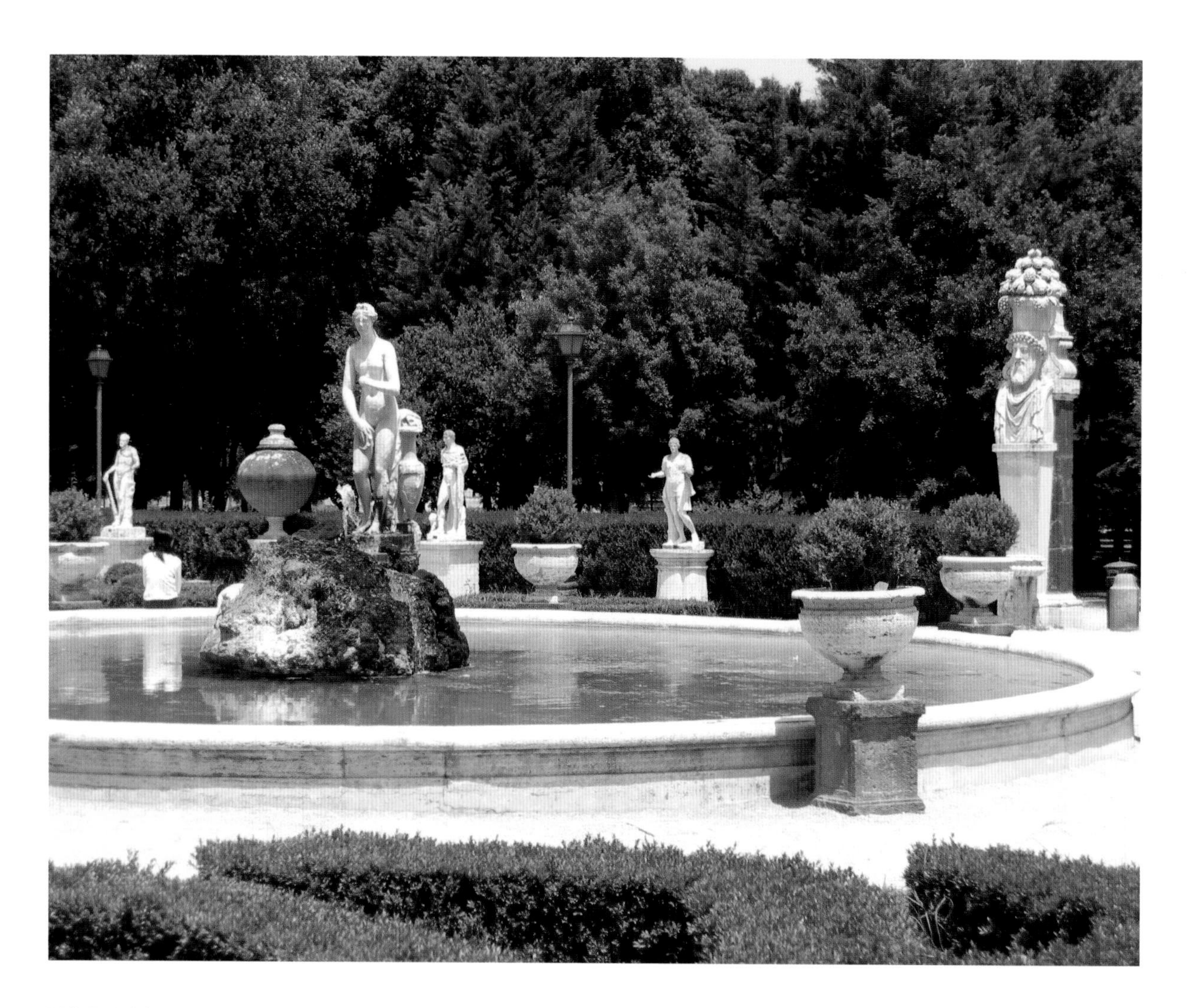

FOUNTAIN, VILLA BORGHESE GARDENS
(above)

Rome's most celebrated open space is a park with attractive gardens allowing visitors a break from the bustle of the city. The gardens also contain several museums, of which the two most important are the Villa Borghese itself, with its outstanding collection of Bernini sculptures, and the Villa Giulia, which contains an exceptional array of Etruscan treasures.

THE ROMAN FORUM
(opposite)

Now a jumble of ruins, the Forum was once the heart of the Roman Empire, a thriving complex of buildings and activity that ruled a considerable part of the Ancient World. This view is through the Arch of Septimius Severus built in the early third century AD to commemorate military victories in what is now Iran. It is situated at the bottom of the Capitoline Hill, one of the famous seven hills of Rome.

THE SPANISH STEPS AND TRINITÀ DEI MONTI

(*opposite*)

The Spanish Steps (Scalinata di Spagna) are a habitual gathering place for the youth of Rome and allegedly for those hoping to be talent-spotted as models by the capital's many artists. The three levels allude to the Holy Trinity, celebrated too in the form of the seventeenth century Trinità dei Monti church at the top of the steps, which offers fine views over the whole of Rome.

FONTANA DI TREVI

(*above*)

Work began on the flamboyant Fontana di Trevi (Trevi Fountain) in 1732 and finished thirty years later, after the initial designer Nicola Salvi had died. Superstitious visitors wishing to return to Rome often drop a coin in the fountain. A favored location for movie directors, it famously features in a scene of Fellini's *La Dolce Vita* in which blonde movie siren Anita Ekberg wades through and splashes herself with water.

THE PALATINE HILL AND CIRCUS MAXIMUS

(*following pages*)

Rome's origins probably lie in this area of the city, now an open air museum and public park. Emperor Augustus was born here, and Romulus and Remus are said to have been discovered by their wolf mother nearby. Numerous emperors had residences on the Palatine Hill, and the ruins of luxury palaces and houses are spread across the surrounds. Directly below the Palatine sit the remains of the Circus Maximus, the first and largest stadium in ancient Rome, where centuries of chariot racing and public games were staged.

LE CENTO FONTANE, VILLA D'ESTE, TIVOLI (*opposite*)

Tivoli, a small town in Lazio, is a mere 25 miles from Rome, and in both Roman and Renaissance times was a popular spot for well-to-do Romans to have their country houses. Converted from a Benedectine monastery in 1550, the Villa d'Este is the most spectacular of these retreats, famous, above all, for its magnificent garden which was built on a steep hill in a series of harmonious terraces. The Cento Fontane (hundred fountains) is one of many outstanding fountains to admire.

TEATRO MARITTIMO, VILLA ADRIANA, TIVOLI (*above*)

The Villa Adriana was the largest and most luxurious of all the villas in the Roman world. Built for the Emperor Hadrian a few years before his death in 138 AD, it covers a huge area and contains many stunning and picturesque ruins. One of the most magical is the Teatro Marittimo, a circular colonnade surrounding a large pool complete with an island where, it is thought, the emperor used to retreat for brief spells of solitude.

PARCO DEI MOSTRI, BOMARZO

(*above*)

A riot of mossy sculptures greets the visitor at every turn at the Parco dei Mostri (Park of Monsters) in the province of Viterbo, which was constructed for the hunchbacked Duke of Orsini in 1552. The thinking behind the commission remains a mystery, but scholars have suspected cheeky parody (of the extremes of Mannerist art) or as possible therapy for the Duke's grief after the death of his wife. The most iconic of these bizarre, fantastic works is the Porta dell'Inferno (Gate of Hell).

THEATER, OSTIA ANTICA

(*opposite*)

Ostia Antica was the original port of ancient Rome until changing sea levels left it stranded about two miles inland. Today it's an easy train ride from Rome and well worth visiting for its outstanding Roman remains. Rebuilt in the second century AD, Ostia's theater had a capacity of 3000–4000 and plays are still performed here. Commanding good views of the ancient town's market square, the Piazzale delle Corporazoni, the theater is also a popular picnic spot.

Southern Italy and the Islands

Campania
Puglia ◆ Basilicata ◆ Calabria
Sicily
Sardinia

SOUTHERN ITALY

Campania

Campania marks the beginning of the true Italian South. Naples is the center of the region possessing distinctive atmosphere and architecture. Its amazing bay offers many spectacular vantage points. Close to the city is the most famous Roman ruin of all, the once-bustling town of Pompeii, both destroyed and preserved by the volcanic ash of Mount Vesuvius over seventeen hundred years ago. Near Naples too is the lower-lying volcanic area of the Campi Flegrei–an area dense with Roman mythological associations–that includes the steaming Solfatara. The beautiful island of Capri (home to the amazing Blue Grotto) and its neighbour Ischia have scenic counterparts south of the city and along the Amalfi Coast, in stunning resorts such as Positano and Sorrento. Here too is the Villa Cimbrone at Ravello with its precipitious views and, south, the picturesque and isolated Hellenic temples of Paestum. To the north lies the astonishing vast palace and gardens of the Reggia di Caserta.

VIA DEI TRIBUNALI, NAPLES

Once the Decumanus Maximus, backbone of the ancient city's grid system, today Via dei Tribunali is the noisy, bustling heart of Naples's historic center. Lined with historic pizzerias and dotted with shrines to the Virgin Mary, the street has plenty of Southern Italian charm. Stalls along the length of the street peddle anything from fruit and vegetables to the local delicacy taralli (salty cracker-type snacks), with the stall holders hawking for business at the tops of their voices.

FRUTTADORO
Doppio Gusto
Prodotti di Sicilia
IMBALLAGGIO ECOLOGICO
PER ALIMENTI

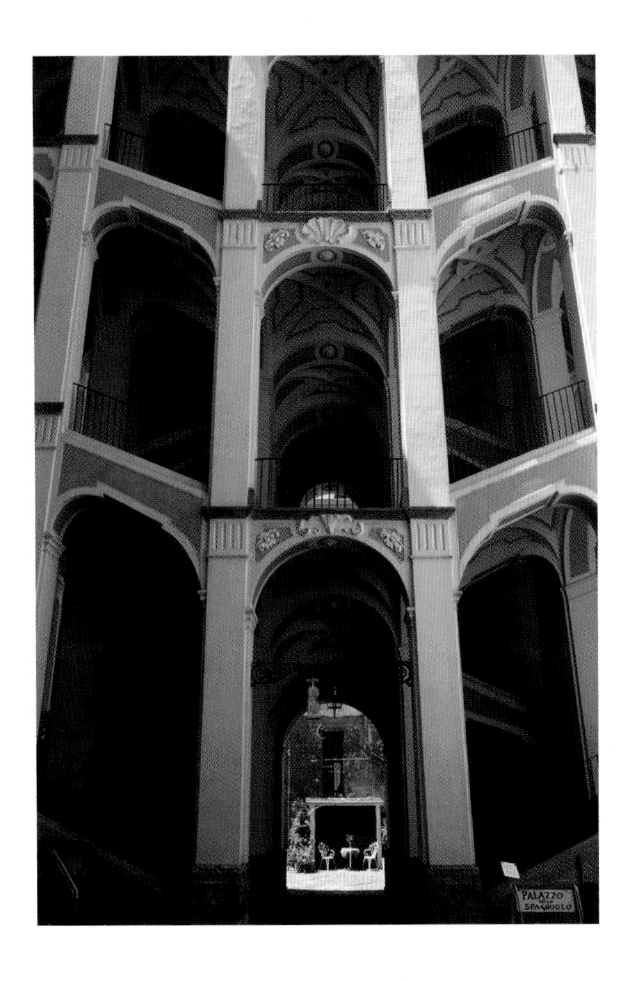

STAIRCASES, PALAZZO DELLO SPAGNUOLO

(*above*)

Along the Via dei Vergini in Naples is the Palazzo dello Spagnuolo, built in 1738. At the back of the Palazzo are two extraordinary staircases that double back on each other, creating one of the city's finest and most unusual examples of Neapolitan Baroque.

CERTOSA E MUSEO DI SAN MARTINO

(*opposite*)

This fourteenth-century monastic complex is now a national museum and one of Naples's most celebrated attractions. It was founded in 1325 by Charles, Duke of Calabria. Among many outstanding features is a baroque cloister; in a corner of it lies a small cemetery for former monks marked out by skulls on a balustrade.

POSITANO
(*opposite*)

The spectacular situation of the small town of Positano on the Amalfi coast is the source of its fame and its status as one of Italy's most exclusive resorts. Actor Tom Cruise is an admirer, as was American novelist John Steinbeck, who praised it as, "a dream place that isn't quite real when you are there and becomes beckoningly real after you have gone."

DESERTED OBSERVATORY, THE SOLFATARA

(*above*)

The Solfatara is the crater of a semi-extinct volcano that often emits jets of steamy, sulphurous fumes. In Roman times it was thought to be to be the mythological home of the god of fire (Vulcan), and to be near the entrance to the underworld (Hades). The Solfatara in the town of Pozzuoli lies within a larger volcanic area, the Campi Flegrei (fiery fields) just west of Naples.

VILLA CIMBRONE, RAVELLO

(*opposite*)

The Villa's belvedere, also named the Terrazzo dell'Infinito, lies beyond a walkway leading to a classical-style temple Its garden is open to the public and was transformed, in the nineteenth century, into a unique combination of English, Moorish and classical styles by Ernest Beckett, an English aristocrat and politician.

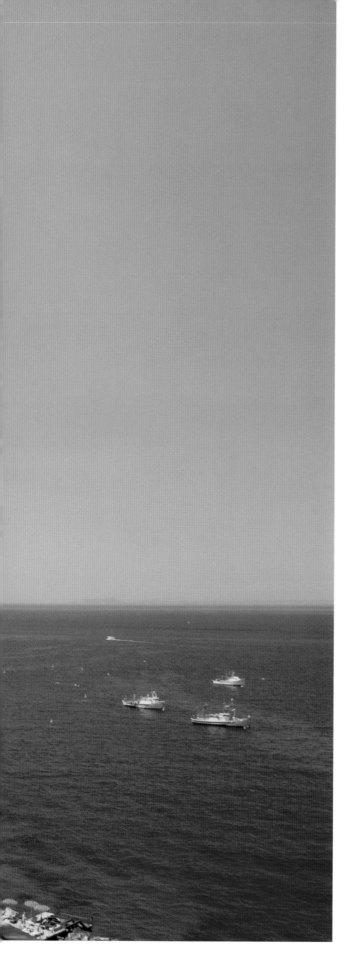

TEMPLE OF NEPTUNE, PAESTUM

(*above*)

The Greeks founded the now-deserted settlement of Paestum south of Salerno in the sixth century BC calling it Poseidonia. The largest temple, built around 450 BC is the most complete of three remaining at a location, which excellent museum aside, is remarkably quiet. Paestum was abandoned in the ninth century due to Saracen invaders and the spread of malaria.

VIEW OF THE BAY OF NAPLES, SORRENTO

(*opposite*)

Sorrento became a destination for upper-class gentlemen on the Grand Tour in the nineteenth century and it has subsequently remained popular with foreign visitors attracted by the town's setting on rocky cliffs and its fine views. The town is also known as a center of production for the popular lemon digestif, limoncello, that can be sampled alongside the fabulous vistas.

POMPEII

(*following pages*)

This is a typical paved street in the large Roman commercial center of Pompeii. Mount Vesuvius—still the only currently active volcano in mainland Europe—was the cause of Pompeii's destruction in AD 79. Lava from an eruption buried the town for about 1700 years before its rediscovery and excavation in the eighteenth and nineteenth ccenturies.

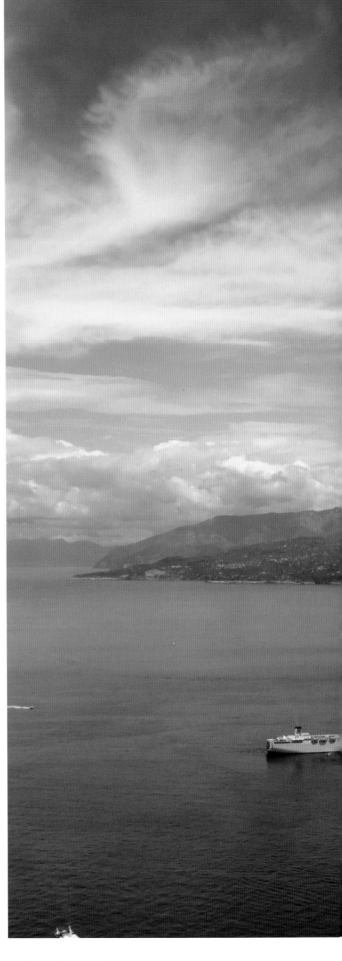

CAPRI, VIEW OVER THE BAY OF NAPLES

(*opposite*)

On a cliff one thousand feet above the sea, this statue of the Roman emperor on the terrace of the luxury Hotel Caesar Augustus has a 360-degree panoramic view. Caesar's gaze can take in Mount Vesuvius, Sorrento, the island of Ischia, and Capri itself as well as the Villa San Michele, a nearby tourist attraction with a similarly priviliged situation.

BLUE GROTTO, CAPRI (*above*)

The dazzling blue of this famous sea cave (Grotta Azzurra) on Capri did not escape the attention of the Emperor Tiberius who is thought to have used it as a sanctuary and swum here, as statues have been discovered at the base of the grotto. Visitors can enter the cave in twos; below the entrance is another hole in the rock where light passes through water and therefore creates the unique intensity of light here.

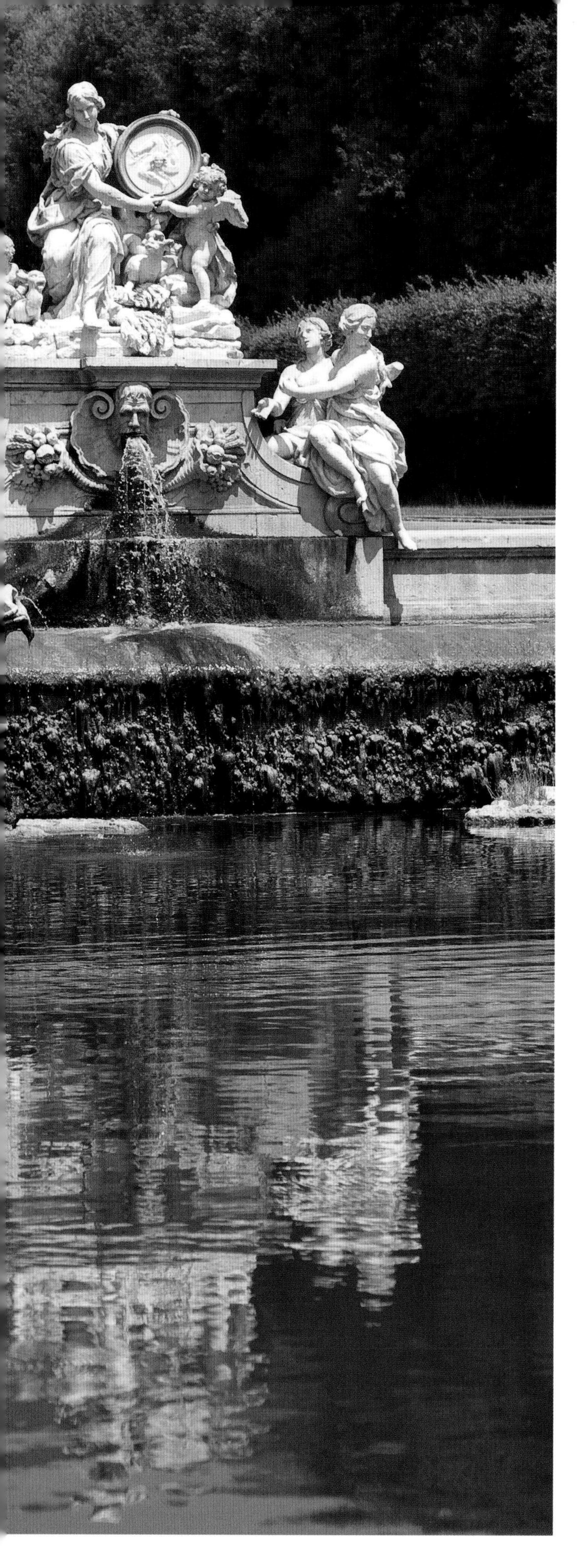

LA FONTANA DI CERERE, REGGIA DI CASERTA

(*opposite*)

The town of Caserta north of Naples is the location of a huge royal complex built in the eighteenth century for the Bourbon King Charles III, giving the town the nickname of the "Versailles of Naples". This fountain, named for the god of agriculture, Ceres, is one of several devoted to mythological themes. It is situated in the royal gardens built behind the Palazzo Reale (home to a staggering 1,200 rooms) along a central axis that is an astounding 1.86 miles long.

SOUTHERN ITALY

Puglia
Basilicata
Calabria

Puglia is the "heel" of Italy, with a long history of foreign invaders from the Greeks onwards. The Holy Roman Empire, dominant in the thirteenth century, left its mark in the region with several Swabian-style castles, the finest being the Castel del Monte, in Andria. Native only to Puglia are the wonderful cone-shaped roofs of *trulli* buildings best observed at Alberobello, whereas charming ports like Trani pull in visitors attracted by the scenery and sun. Most appealing of the resorts in Basilicata's Tyrrhenian coast might be the promontory town of Tropea, but the most atmospheric settlement in the region is probably Matera, with its terraced cave dwellings and churches called *sassi* gouged out of a forbidding stony landscape. Another legacy of former times in Calabria is the Catolica di Stilo, a charming example of Byzantine style from the ninth century.

ALBEROBELLO, LE MURGE

The conical, tapering roofs of the cylindrical buildings known as *trulli* dot the landscape of the Murge region. The UNESCO World Heritage Site of Alberobello is the best place to explore these strange structures—unique to this part of Puglia—with over 1500 crowding the town's narrow streets. Their original purpose is unknown but they now serve mostly as shops. There are also *trulli* restaurants, and guesthouses, and even a *trulli* cathedral.

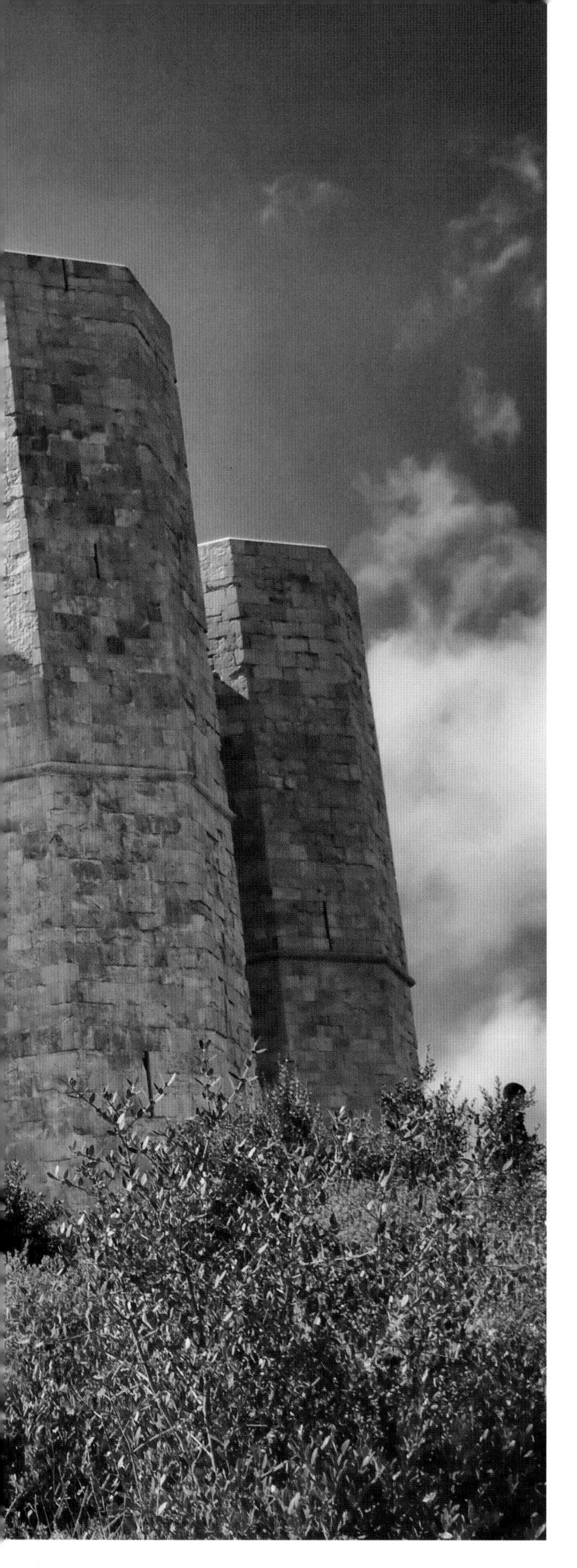

TRANI
(above)

Trani's Norman Duomo, situated close to the sea, was mostly built between 1159 and 1186 using the cream-colored limestone of the region, though there had been a church on the site since the seventh century. It is dedicated to San Nicola Pellegrino—a little-remembered miracle worker of the eleventh century. The austere facade is lifted by the pretty rose window, and the unusual Gothic arch beneath the bell tower.

CASTEL DEL MONTE
(opposite)

Remote in the expansive plains near Ruvo di Puglia, the thirteenth-century Castel del Monte outshines all of Frederick II's many fortifications. It is also one of the most sophisticated and precisely planned secular buildings of the Middle Ages: a harmonious geometrical study, with eight vaulted rooms on each of two floors, overlooking a central courtyard.

CATTOLICA DI STILO
(*above*)

Under Byzantine rule, Stilo was one of the most important towns in the region, and its hillside caves became a center for Basilian monks. It was they who built the distinctive ninth-century Cattolica (the word derives from the Greek *katholiki*, referring to churches with a baptistry), whose five domes overlook the town from a ledge on the flank of Monte Consolino. It remains one of the finest examples of Byzantine religious architecture in Italy.

SASSI, MATERA
(*opposite*)

The *sassi* (caves) that pocked the ravine above the Gravina river are thought to have provided refuge for the monks of the Byzantine empire. Many of their chapels—gouged out of the rock—were taken over by peasants in the fifteenth century, and a cave-dwelling town evolved. By the eighteenth century some of the buildings fronting the caves had grown into large mansions, convents, and churches; now a major draw for tourists, the area is also a UNESCO World Heritage Site.

SANTA MARIA DELL'ISOLA, TROPEA
(*previous pages*)

Perhaps the highlight of the southern Tyrrhenian coast is the resort of Tropea. The monastery of Santa Maria perches on a rock below the upper town; fishermens' caves are strung out along the path towards the church. On a clear day the island of Stromboli is sometimes visible from the high vantage points of the town.

SOUTHERN ITALY

Sicily

The island of Sicily, the largest in the Mediterranean, is arguably the Italian region with the strongest sense of its own identity. Much of its landscape is wild and rugged, with Mount Etna a looming presence over settlements such as Castiglione di Sicilia. Though economically poor, Sicily is culturally rich with a diversity that reflects its regular colonization over the centuries. The Ancient Greeks, in particular, made a stong impact and the island boasts several impressive remains–among them the Valle dei Templi (Valley of the Temples) at Agrigento and the well-preserved theater at Taormina. The Byzantines, Arabs and Normans also made their mark, and much of Sicily's medieval architecture, such as the magnificent cathedrals of Cefalù and Monreale, combine elements from these different cultures. There are also a wealth of Baroque buildings, a result of the devastating earthquake of 1693. Beach lovers also have plenty to choose from, not just on Sicily itself but on the many nearby smaller islands.

CASTIGLIONE DI SICILIA

In the shadow of Mount Etna lies the charming mountain town of Castiglione di Sicilia in the province of Catania. In the valley below there is a remarkable Byzantine chapel built out of lava known as "LaCuba" because of its regular and harmonious proportions, that dates from the eighth century. The splendid views vie for the visitor's attention with delicious local cheeses made from sheep's milk.

+ FACTVS HOMO FACTOR HOMINIS FACTIQ REDEMPTOR + IVDICO

TEATRO GRECO, TAORMINA

(*previous pages*)

Carved from the hillside and offering a truly spectacular view of the snow-topped summit of Mount Etna, the Teatro Greco (Greek Theater) is one of Sicily's most impressive monuments. Despite its name, most of the remaining structure was rebuilt by the Romans in the first century AD as a gladiatorial arena. Nearby, the beach at Mazzarò—accessible from Taormina by cable car—is famous for the tiny Isola Bella, a small island barely separated from the mainland which is now a nature reserve.

DUOMO DI CEFALÙ

(*opposite*)

Situated on a promontory backed by a great outcrop of rock, the coastal town of Cefalù makes a dramatic impact, especially when approached from the sea. Though a settlement since Greek times, it was the Normans who really left their mark there. The magnificent Romanesque Duomo, with its imposing twin towers, was begun in 1131 on the orders of King Roger II. It contains some remarkable Byzantine-style mosaics, dominated by the imposing figure of Christ Pantocrator, one hand raised in blessing, the other holding an open Bible.

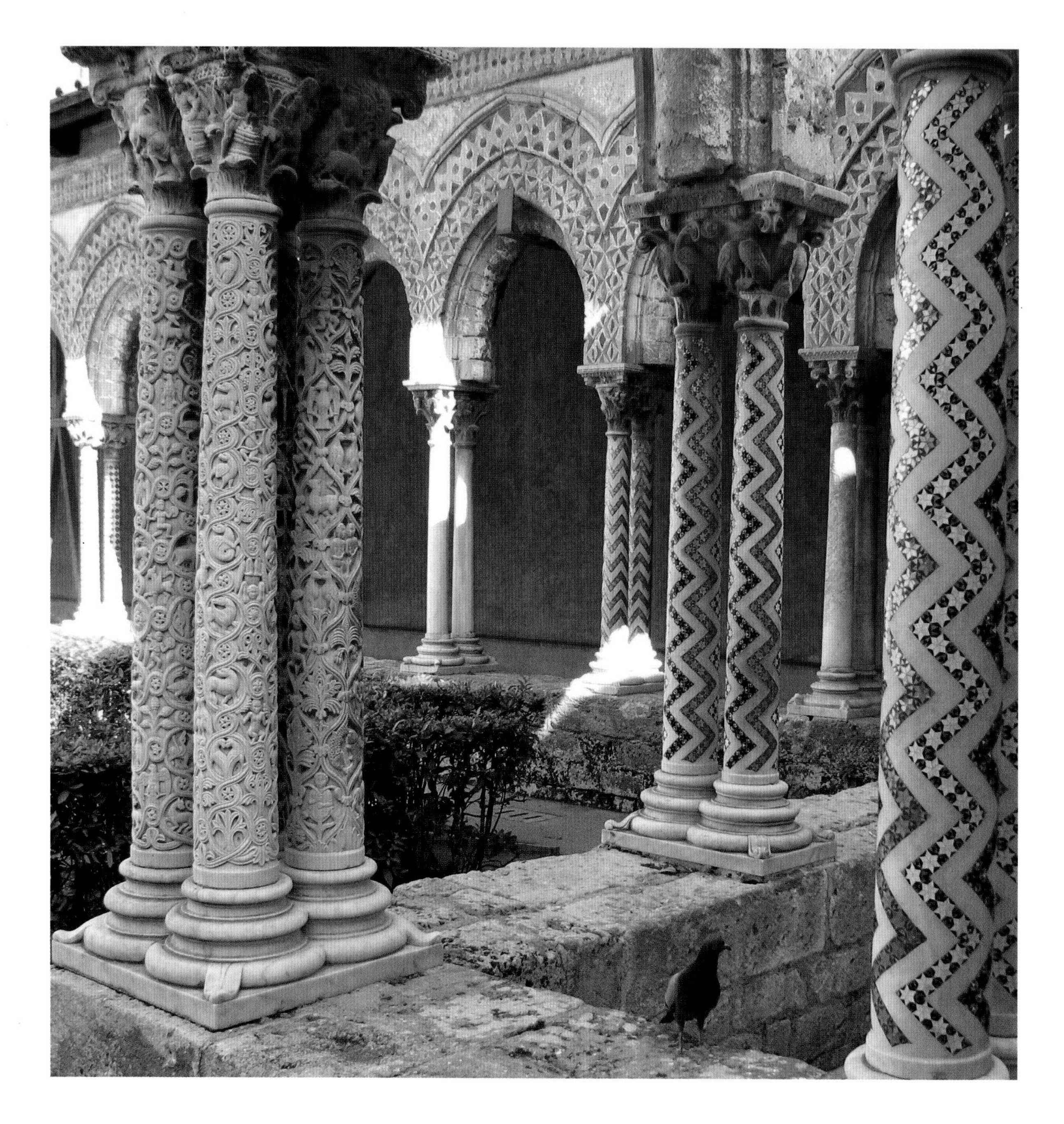

CHIOSTRO DEI BENEDETTINI, DUOMO DI MONREALE

(*above*)

A few miles southwest of Sicily's capital, Palermo, is the delightful town of Monreale. King William II commissioned its glorious Duomo, with the intention of rivaling the one at Palermo. The building and its adjacent Benedictine monastery were completed in 1182. The highly original architecture successfully combines a mix of Norman, Moorish, and Byzantine influences, nowhere more strikingly than in the beautiful cloister, with its richly decorated double columns and pointed arches.

TEMPIO DELLA CONCORDIA, VALLE DEI TEMPLI, AGRIGENTO

(*opposite*)

To the south of the town of Agrigento are the remains of the original Greek settlement, Akragas, founded in the sixth century AD. The Valle dei Templi (Valley of the Temples) houses the town's many remarkable religious buildings, the best preserved of which is the so-called Tempio della Concordia (Temple of Concord). Dating from around 430 BC, all its 34 Doric columns—made from the local honey-colored sandstone—are intact, and the overall effect is both beautiful and harmonious.

FARAGLIONI, TONNARA DI SCOPELLO

(*opposite*)

The ancient tuna fishery next to Scopello is home to several unusual *faraglioni,* or rock towers, which are topped by a type of prickly pear cactus. The *tonnara* is set within its own cove, and its photogenic appeal has attracted the directors of advertisements and feature films including Steven Soderbergh who used it as a setting for *Ocean's Twelve* (2004).

MARINA CORTA, LÍPARI

(*above*)

The island of Lípari is an excellent base for exploring the Aeolian islands of the region. The Marina Corta to the south of the town's historical citadel is Lípari's historic harbor, but nowadays is the quieter of the island's two embarkation points. Colorful fishing boats and vessels used mainly for short excursions predominate here, so it is an excellent spot to enjoy the relaxed small-town atmosphere and watch the world go by.

SOUTHERN ITALY

Sardinia

Few places in Europe display quite such a diverse array of cultural and historic influences as Sardinia. In Nora in the island's southwest can be found the ruins of foreign occupiers such as the Carthaginians and Phoenicians, not to mention the ancient Romans. The island also retains a strong sense of its own identity which is reflected in traditional local costumes and the distinctive type of prehistoric building, called *nuraghe.* Sardinia is not short on natural wonders, either. The coast is a beguiling mix of translucent waters, isolated coves, and spectacular cliffs such as those at Masu in the southwest or Capo Caccia in the northwest. Sardinia's many towns are worth a visit with busy Cagliari in the south and Alghero in the north, two of the most immediately attractive to the eye. In the northwest the unspoiled town of Bosa beside the banks of the River Temo has retained its own self-contained and particularly Sardinian charm.

ALGHERO

The original Ligurian and Sardinian occupants of Alghero were so thoroughly expelled by Spanish settlers after 1353 that today the look and feel of the town remain distinctly Spanish—the Catalan language has even been enjoying a revival here in recent years. Alghero's atmospheric old town, filled with labyrinthine alleys and cobbled streets, is the principal attraction for tourists, but down at the harbor, the town also enjoys a flourishing fishing industry.

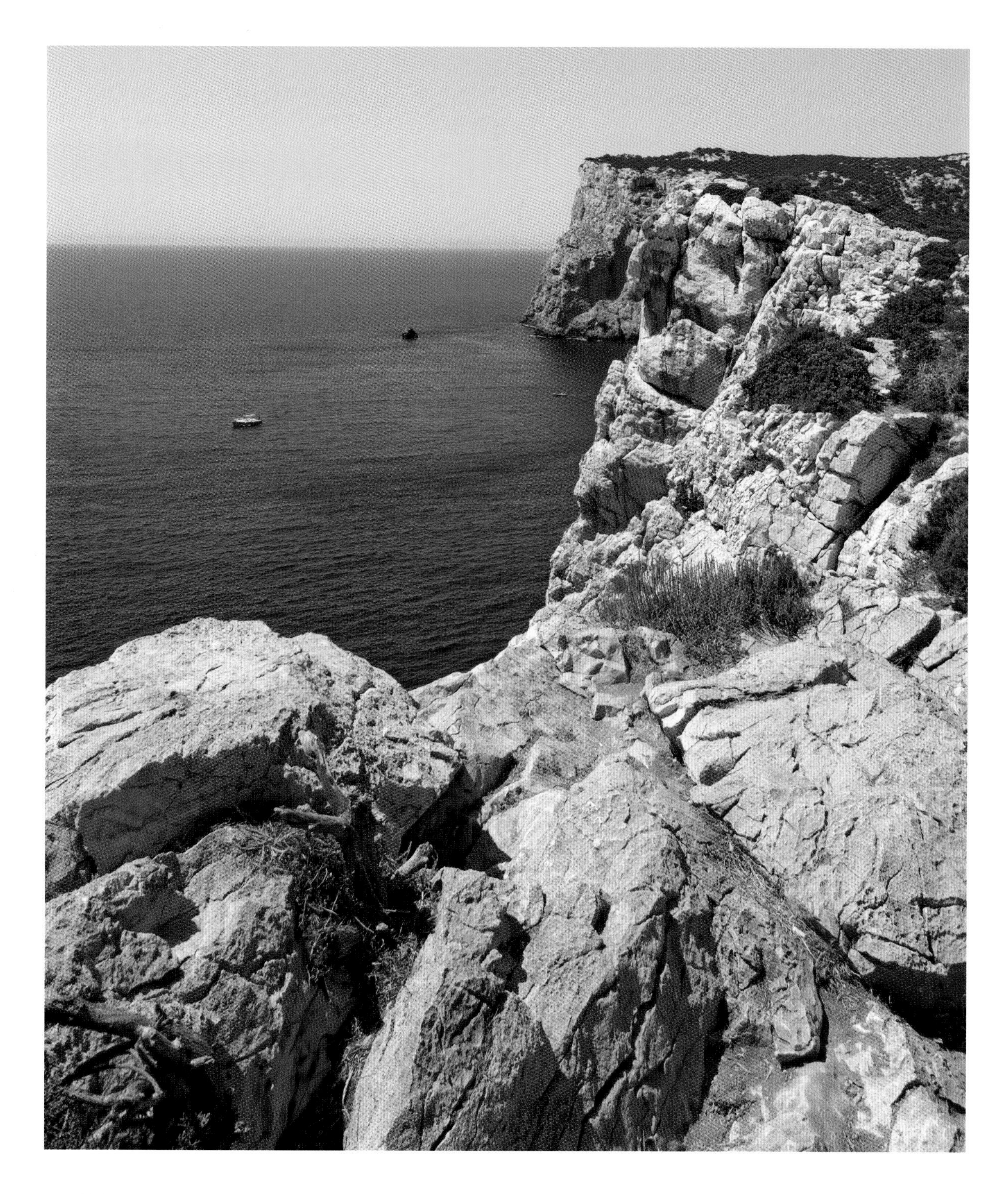

BASTIONE SAN REMY, CAGLIARI

(*opposite*)

Without doubt the most evocative entrance to Cagliari's old Castello quarter, the Bastione San Remy is in fact a relatively recent nineteenth-century addition to the city's ancient walls. Those who trek up the stairs within the Arco di Trionfo (Triumphal Arch) are rewarded with outstanding views across the port, lagoons, and countryside without, and of the historic citadel within.

CAPO CACCIA

(*above*)

The magnificent limestone cliffs of Capo Caccia on a remote peninsula in northwestern Sardinia, are famous not just for their striking appearance: beneath their gnarled exterior they conceal a labyrinth of caves. Among the most famous is the Grotta di Nettuno, (Neptune's Grotto), a two-and-a-half mile network replete with dramatically shaped stalactites and stalagmites.

TRADITIONAL DRESS, OLIENA

(*above*)

The traditional dress of Sardinia—brimming with elaborate embroidery and displaying Italian, Spanish, and Moorish influences—remains an important aspect of island life, particularly at festivals. Female costumes differ greatly from place to place (hundreds of styles can be seen across Sardinia), but these women of the Oliena region wear the long shawl, pleated skirt, embroidered shirts, and colorful ornamentation that are common to them all.

NORA, CAGLIARI

(*opposite*)

Situated at the tip of a peninsula twenty miles from Cágliari, Nora was Sardinia's first town. Its rich history—founded by Phoenician sailors and merchants on an existing Sard settlement and later controlled by Carthage and Rome before being abandoned around the third century AD—has left a wealth of archaeological remains on this atmospheric site, including well-preserved mosaics, temples, houses, and Carthaginian warehouses.

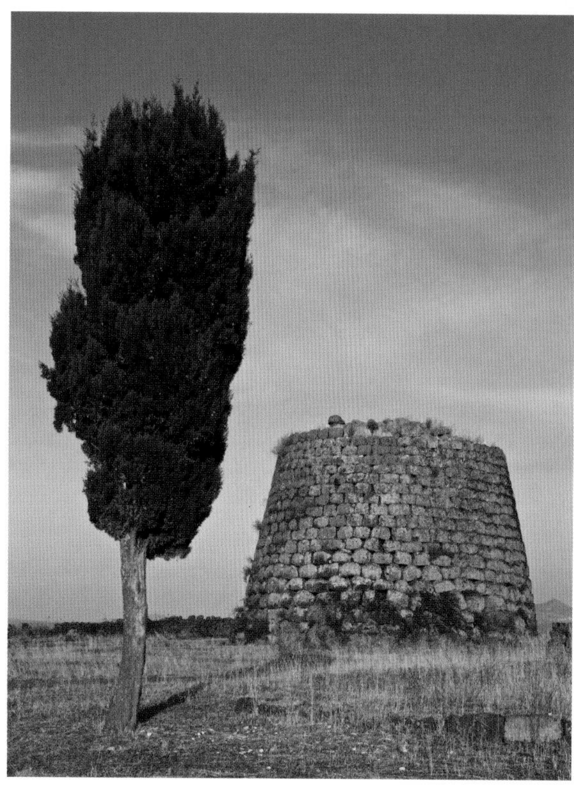

NURAGHE AT SILANUS (*above*)

Perhaps the most dominant feature in the Sardinian landscape are the ubiquitous nuraghi—seven thousand or so of these truncated stone structures dot the island. They date from 1800 to 300 BC and were built with basalt blocks without bonding. We know very little about the nuraghic people who made them, though they were clearly consummate engineers. Some nuraghi were small fortresses, while others were houses, temples, tombs, or even theaters.

RIVERSIDE AT BOSA (*opposite*)

At the mouth of the Temo river sits the picture-perfect town of Bosa. Its pastel houses begin at the waterfront; from there they struggle up the hillside to the Castello Malaspina through the medieval Sa Costa district whose mazy, cobbled lanes have changed little over the centuries.

Index

Picture credits

All images © Dorling Kindersley and Rough Guides except the following:

PART ONE: *Northern Italy*

pp.10–11 Geislerspitzen, Dolomites © Gavin Hellier/JAI/Corbis; pp.54–55 Fishing for wine bottles during a festival in Alba © Franz–Marc Frei/Corbis; pp.58–59 Climbers watching top of Mont Blanc from peak over Courmayeur © Angelo Cavalli/Corbis; pp.60–61 View of the old city, Genoa (Genova), Italy © Corbis – All Rights Reserved; p.63 San Remo Beach © gsmcity/Fotolia; pp.72–3 Castello di Torrechiara, Parma © maurosessanta/Fotolia; p.74 Castell'Arquato © Ettore/Fotolia; p.75 Ponte Vecchio, Bobbio © m.bonotto/Fotolia;

PART TWO: *Central Italy*

pp.86–7 Palazzo Ducale, Urbino © prescott09/Fotolia; p.90 Saepinum © De Agostini/Getty Images; p.104 Leaning Tower of Pisa © Robert Hoetink/Fotolia; p.129 Piano Grande di Castelluccio © Joe Gough/Fotolia; pp.142–3 The Palatine Hill and Circus Maximus © zardo/Fotolia;

PART THREE: *Southern Italy and the Islands*

pp.154–5 Positano © puchu/Fotolia; pp.160–1 Pompeii © ProMotion/Fotolia; pp.162–3 Capri, View over the Bay of Naples © 2010 Andy Martin Jr/Fotolia; pp.164–5 La Fontana di Cerere, Reggia di Caserta © Maurizio Malangone/Fotolia; pp.166–7 Alberobello, Le Murge © Claudio Colombo/Fotolia; pp.168–9 Castel del Monte © Gabriela/Fotolia; p.169 Trani © Lusso Adv/Fotolia; pp.170–1 Santa Maria dell'Isola, Tropea © Richard Broadwell/Beateworks/Corbis; 172–3 Sassi, Matera © fotografiche.eu/Fotolia; pp.178–9 Duomo di Cefalù © V. Zhuravlev/Fotolia; p.180 Chiostro dei benedettini, Duomo di Monreale © Richard/Fotolia; pp.184–5 Alghero © The Factory/Fotolia; p.189 Ruins, Nora © Fyle/Fotolia; pp.190–1 Riverside at Bosa © diego cervo/Fotolia; p.191 Nuraghe at Silanus © orzocco/Fotolia.

Cover and pp. 2–3 View over Assisi town: © Ros Edwards/Alamy